Building Up One Another

Gene A. Getz

While this book is designed for the reader's personal use and profit, it is also intended for group study. A leader's guide is available from your local bookstore or from the publisher.

VICTOR BOOKS a division of SP Publications, Inc.

WHEATON. ILLINOIS 60187

Offices also in
Whitby, Ontario, Canada
Amersham-on-the-Hill, Bucks, England

Other Victor books by Gene Getz:

Loving One Another
Encouraging One Another
Praying for One Another
Serving One Another
Sharpening the Focus of the Church

Seventeenth printing, 1984

Library of Congress Catalog Card No. 76-19918
ISBN: 0-88207-744-9

Victor Books
A division of SP Publications, Inc.
Wheaton, Ill. 60187

Contents

Looking Forward

Again and again, New Testament writers exhorted believers to engage in specific activities that would enable the body of Christ to function effectively and to grow spiritually. Frequently they used a unique word to describe this mutual and reciprocal process—the Greek word *allēlōn*, most frequently translated "one another." In fact, excluding the Gospels, the word is used 58 times in the New Testament. Paul leads the list for frequency, having used the word 40 times.

Obviously, certain of these concepts and injunctions are repeated from letter to letter. But when all the "one another" exhortations are studied carefully, and grouped together according to specific meanings, they can be reduced to approximately 12 significant actions Christians are to take toward "one another" to help build up the body of Christ.

This is what this book is about. It includes 12 chapters built around these powerful exhortations. You'll find it more than just a study of what these injunctions mean. Each chapter includes a practical section: a series of steps for putting these exhortations into action in your local church.

These practical sections represent more than mere theory. They have been tried and tested. They work. When these injunctions are not only talked about but applied, you'll be involved in one of the most dynamic forces on earth—the functioning body of Jesus Christ.

Renewal—A Biblical Perspective

Renewal is the essence of dynamic Christianity and the basis on which Christians, both in a corporate or "body" sense and as individual believers, can determine the will of God. Paul made this clear when he wrote to the Roman Christians—"be transformed by the *renewing of your mind*." Then he continued "you will be able to test and approve what God's will is" (Rom. 12:2). Here Paul is talking about renewal in a corporate sense. In other words, Paul is asking these Christians as a *body* of believers, to develop the mind of Christ through corporate renewal.

Personal renewal will not happen as God intended it unless it happens in the context of corporate renewal. On the other hand, corporate renewal will not happen as God intended without personal renewal. Both are necessary.

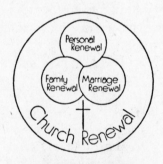

Biblical Renewal
Developing the mind of Christ

The larger circle represents "church renewal." This is the most comprehensive concept in the New Testament. However, every local church is made up of smaller self-contained, but interrelated units. The *family* in Scripture emerges as the "church in miniature." In turn, the family is made up of an even smaller social unit—*marriage*. The third inner circle represents *personal* renewal, which is inseparably linked to all of the other basic units. Marriage is made up of two separate individuals who become one. The family is made up of parents and children,who are also to reflect the mind of Christ. And the church is made up of not only individual Christians, but couples and families.

Though all of these social units are interrelated, biblical renewal can begin within any specific social unit. But wherever it begins—in the church, families, marriages, or individuals—the process immediately touches all the other social units. And one thing is certain! All that God says is consistent and harmonious. He does not have one set of principles for the church and another set for the family, another for husbands and wives and another for individual Christians. For example, the principles God outlines for local church elders, fathers,and husbands regarding their role as leaders are interrelated and consistent. If they are not, we can be sure that we have not interpreted God's plan accurately.

The books listed below are part of the Biblical Renewal Series by Gene Getz designed to provide supportive help in moving toward renewal. They all fit into one of the circles described here and will provoke thought, provide interaction and tangible steps toward growth.

"ONE ANOTHER" SERIES	PERSONALITY SERIES	THE "MEASURE OF" SERIES
Building Up	Abraham	Measure of a . . .
One Another	David	Church
Encouraging	Joseph	Family
One Another	Joshua	Man
Loving	Moses	Marriage
One Another	Nehemiah	Woman
Praying for	Elijah	Christian—Philippians
One Another		Christian—Titus
Serving		Christian—James 1
One Another		

Sharpening the Focus of the Church presents an overall perspective for Church Renewal. All of these books are available from your bookstore.

1

Members of One Another

"So we who are many, are one body in Christ, and individually *members one of another*" (Rom. 12:5, NASB).

The New Testament clearly and unequivocally states that Christians are "members of one another." All New Testament authors recognized this truth. But it was Paul who developed the concept extensively in his correspondence with certain churches. It was also Paul who exclusively used a unique illustration to get his point across—the human body. In his letters to the Romans, the Corinthians, the Ephesians, and the Colossians, he penned the word "body" (*soma*) more than 30 times to illustrate the functioning church. Approximately half of the times he used the word, he was referring to the human, physical body with its many parts and members. In the other half, he applied the term to the Church—the body of Christ.

The Analogy
Paul's most extensive use of the analogy of the human body appears in his letter to the Corinthians, no doubt because of

their carnality and immaturity. Because of their immature state, he made a special effort to clearly and carefully spell out the similarity between the "human body" and "Christ's body—the Church." In two extensive paragraphs, he used the word "body" 13 times to illustrate just *how* this body actually functions. Paul didn't want them to miss his point! And since he had previously experienced their inability to grasp spiritual truth, and since they were still unable to handle "solid food" (1 Cor. 3:1-2), he decided to make his point so clear that even the most immature Christian could understand what he was illustrating. Thus he wrote:

Now the *body* [the human body] is not made up of one part but of many.

If the foot should say, "Because I am not a hand, I do not belong to the *body*," it would not for that reason cease to be a part of the *body*.

And if the ear should say, "Because I am not an eye, I do not belong to the *body*," it would not for that reason cease to be a part of the *body*.

If the whole *body* were an eye, where would the sense of hearing be? If the whole *body* were an ear, where would the sense of smell be? But in fact God has arranged the parts in the *body*, everyone of them, just as He wanted them to be. If they were all one part, where would the *body* be? As it is, there are many parts, but one *body*.

The eye cannot say to the hand, "I don't need you!" And the head cannot say to the feet, "I don't need you!" On the contrary, those parts of the *body* that seem to be weaker are indispensable, and the parts of the *body* that we think are less honorable we treat with special honor. And the parts that are unpresentable are treated with special modesty, while our presentable parts need no special treatment. But God has combined the members of the *body* and has given greater honor to the parts that lacked it, so that there should be no division in the *body,* but that its parts should have equal concern for each other. If one part suffers, every part suffers with it; if one part is honored, every part rejoices with it (1 Cor. 12:14-26).

There was no way that even the most carnal and immature Corinthian Christian could miss Paul's message. If repetition with variety is a significant key to learning (and it is), Paul certainly was a master teacher. His point of application was that Christians are "members one of another." Thus he concluded these lengthy, descriptive, and repetitious paragraphs by adding this concise statement: "Now you are the *body of Christ,* and each one of you is a part of it" (1 Cor. 12:27).

A Wrong Emphasis

Three major passages in Paul's letters illustrate and describe the functioning body of Christ. One we've already looked at—1 Corinthians 12. The others are Romans 12 and Ephesians 4.

It is my opinion that many Christians (including myself), who have read and studied these passages of Scripture, have missed Paul's major emphasis. For years I used these passages to teach that Christians must *search for* and *try to discover* their spiritual gifts in order to function in the body of Christ. The reason, of course, is obvious. In all of these passages Paul made extensive reference to specific spiritual gifts.

However, it suddenly dawned on me one day as I was studying that nowhere in these verses can we find any exhortation for individual Christians to "look for" or to "try to discover" his or her spiritual gift or gifts. In fact, *nowhere* in the Bible can we find any such exhortation.

What, then, was Paul saying?

First, Paul was teaching the New Testament believers that *no individual Christian can function effectively by himself.*

Not long ago a speck of dust blew into my eye. Instinctively I rubbed my eye with my finger. I didn't have to debate with my finger to help my eye. After pulling the lid down, causing the eye to cry, the dust was washed out. In a short time my eye was back to normal. But without my hand, including specially functioning fingers, the irritant would have remained.

Just as "there are many parts of one body" in the physical makeup of human beings, so the body of Christ is made up of many members. And each member is important. We are indeed "members of one another." No member of Christ's body can say, "I don't need you." We all need each other.

Second, Paul was also teaching that *no member of Christ's body should feel he is more important than another member of Christ's body.* No Christian has exclusive rights to God's grace. This, perhaps, is one of Paul's major teachings in these three passages. His emphasis is on *humility!* Though implied all the way through the Corinthian passage (some Corinthians were saying, "I don't need you" and "I'm more important than you"), Paul made it clear in his Roman letter when he wrote:

"For by the grace given to me I say to every one of you: *Do not think of yourself more highly than you ought, but rather think of yourself with sober judgment,* in accordance with the measure of faith God has given you" (Rom. 12:3).

Then Paul went on to emphasize: "So in Christ we who are many form one body, and each member belongs to all the others" (Rom. 12:5). It seems that the Romans were having a problem similar to the Corinthians', but probably not to the same degree. Some were carnal in their attitudes about their spiritual gifts, using them in such a way so as to make other members of the body feel unimportant.

Interestingly, the Ephesian passage describing "body function" reflects the same emphasis. Setting the stage for the purpose of gifts (as spelled out in Ephesians 4:11-16), Paul wrote: "Be completely *humble* and *gentle; be patient,* bearing with one another in love" (Eph. 4:2).

Why did Paul emphasize humility, gentleness, and patience? Because, as he went on to say, "there is *one body* and *one Spirit*" (Eph. 4:4). With this statement he is in essence saying the same thing he said to the Corinthians: "For we were all baptized *by one Spirit* into *one body* (1 Cor. 12:13). In other words, no member of Christ's body is more important than the other. Though one person may have a more responsible position, in God's sight even the person who may go unnoticed is just as important and necessary in the body of Christ (1 Cor. 12:22-23).

When we use the analogy of the human body, immediately our minds picture the expressive parts of the body: mouth, hands, feet, eyes—the outwardly movable. But the hidden parts: bones, ligaments, muscles, glands—these are also vital to proper functioning. Could the hands or feet or tongue operate without controlling muscles and the all-controlling brain?

Third, Paul was teaching that *Christians should work hard at creating unity in the body of Christ.* This is why Paul wrote clearly to the Corinthians: "The body is a *unit,* though it is made up of many parts" (1 Cor. 12:12). This is why he immediately opened the letter to them by saying, "I appeal to you, brothers, in the name of our Lord Jesus Christ, that *all of you agree with one another* so that there may be *no divisions* among you and that you may be *perfectly united* in mind and thought" (1 Cor. 1:10). And this is why he wrote to the Ephesians, in the very same passage where he discussed body functions: *"Make every effort* to keep the *unity of the Spirit* through the *bond of peace"* (Eph. 4:3).

To sum up, then, what Paul was teaching in these passages is this: Not one of us can function effectively by ourselves; we need each other. Not one of us is more important than any other Christian, even though one of us may have a more obvious or more significant position in the body. We are to be clothed with humility, remembering that even the one who has the greatest responsibility is to be the greatest servant. And finally, all of us as members of Christ's body are to strive diligently for unity and peace. We are to do everything possible to keep misunderstandings from arising and divisions from erupting.

What About Spiritual Gifts?

Paul makes reference to spiritual gifts in each of these passages. In all three instances, no reference or implication is made to indicate these Christians did not know what their gifts were. They knew only too well what gifts they had. Their problem—they were using them incorrectly. Some were building themselves up or putting other Christians down. Some were giving the impression they were more important than others. They didn't need other members of the body. Some who knew they had the "unnoticed" gifts were feeling unimportant in Christ's body.

It would seem that all these gifts, given by the Holy Spirit to the Early Church, were sovereignly and divinely bestowed abilities. Each gift was so obvious that every Christian knew exactly what his gift was. Every Christian also knew immediately what other Christians' gifts were. No one had to go around looking and searching for his gift or gifts. Rather, the problem was how to use it in a humble, gentle, and patient way, realizing that the gift was given not to glorify self, but to minister to others.

What About Spiritual Gifts Today?

Many different opinions about the subject exist in the Church. There is general agreement among most Christian leaders who speak out on the subject, yet many excellent Bible students disagree with each other on some aspects. Significantly, most disagree on how many gifts are yet in existence, how to recognize and discover those that are in existence, and how to use them.

The primary reason for this disagreement seems to be that we are emphasizing something the Bible does not emphasize. As was stated before, nowhere do the Scriptures teach that we as individuals are to look for and to try to discover our gifts before we can function as members in Christ's body.

Some Christians use 1 Corinthians 14:1 to teach that we should try to discover personal spiritual gifts. But a careful look at the text and context strongly points to the fact that this is not what Paul was teaching. All the way through this section of the Corinthian letter, Paul was directing his exhortations not to individuals but to the corporate body of believers at Corinth. He specifically used the second person plural: "Eagerly [as a body] desire spiritual gifts" (1 Cor. 14:1). In other words, *as a body of believers* desire that the greater gifts be manifested in your midst, not the lesser gifts. You see, some Corinthian believers were giving primary attention to "tongues speaking" (definitely classified by Paul as a lesser gift) rather than to apostleship, prophecy, and teaching, which were the "greater gifts" (see 1 Cor. 12:28-31).

The Proper Emphasis

What then does the Bible emphasize? Its emphasis is on becoming mature in Christ. This, of course, was Paul's primary concern in the Corinthian letter—the Corinthian believers were to no longer talk, think, and reason like children (1 Cor. 13:11). Love for others is the most significant key to unity and effective body function.

Furthermore, when Paul discussed the qualifications for

leadership in the church (both for elders and deacons) he made no reference whatever to spiritual gifts. Rather, he wrote extensively about character traits: being above reproach, morally pure, temperate, prudent, respectable, hospitable, being able to teach, not being addicted to wine, not self-willed, not quick-tempered, not pugnacious, uncontentious, gentle, free from the love of money, a good manager of the home, a good reputation with non-Christians, loving what is good, being just, devout. He also stated that church leaders were not to be new converts, for a new convert could not possibly be a *mature* Christian (1 Tim. 3; Titus 1).

Some have interpreted "being able to teach," mentioned in 1 Timothy 3, as the gift of teaching. However, a careful look at the word translated "able to teach" in the original text, and Paul's use of it in 1 Timothy 3:2 and 2 Timothy 2:24, reveals significant evidence that Paul was talking about a quality of life, not a particular pedagogical skill or a special gift. Furthermore, it would be rather strange for Paul to single out the "gift of teaching" as a requirement for leadership and to omit "the gift of pastor" and the "gift of administration." This would be especially strange in view of the fact that Paul definitely instructed elders to be responsible for the teaching, shepherding, and managing responsibilities of a church.

A Personal Experience
For a number of years I diligently taught that Christians should try to discover their spiritual gifts in order to function in the body of Christ. But little by little, I began to notice some serious problems in the lives of those who sat under my teaching—and the teaching of others who took this approach. For one thing, many became confused. Some tried diligently and desperately to find their gifts—to "pigeonhole" what they thought was a spiritual gift given to them at conversion.

But many Christians—including many mature believers—could not seem to isolate their gifts. I remember one pastor who became frustrated because his most mature members were unable to discover for sure what their gifts were.

Another category of people emerges from an emphasis on discovering gifts—those who quickly fixate on what they think their gift is. They promptly begin to use it as a rationalization for not fulfilling other biblical responsibilities. Interestingly enough, I've seen this happen in the context of a theological seminary. For example, a person concludes he has the gift of teaching (not pastoring). This conclusion is based primarily upon the fact that he "feels" comfortable behind a lectern or a pulpit, but feels uncomfortable working with people one-on-one. On the other hand, there's the person who has a difficult time studying, preparing messages, and speaking, but who feels comfortable "hanging loose with people." He concludes, "I have the gift of pastoring, but not of teaching." And, of course, we've all met people who do not share their faith because they know "they don't have the gift of evangelism." Their criterion? They don't feel *comfortable* sharing Christ.

Martin was an excellent Greek and Hebrew student. He loudly proclaimed to fellow seminarians he had the gift of teaching. Evangelism wasn't his calling. He'd spend his life building the lives of believers. Others could evangelize. That was for those who couldn't think deep thoughts . . . or expound the Scriptures!

A little insight into human personality clearly focuses the problem. What this points to is not a lack of gifts but psychological hang-ups, a kind of rationalization that keeps a person from becoming mature in Jesus Christ.

Another problem I have observed resulting from an emphasis on discovering gifts is the problem of self-deception. I'm speaking primarily of the person who thinks he has a gift when he doesn't. For example, the person who has a "quick mind" concludes he has the gift of wisdom. Or the impressionable person given over to "subjective and intuitive thoughts" or even "obsessions" easily concludes he has the gift of prophecy. And so it goes.

These observations drove me back to a fresh study of the New Testament regarding spiritual gifts. To my surprise—and chagrin—I discovered no emphasis on personally looking for spiritual gifts. Rather, I found a profuse and repetitious emphasis on becoming mature in Jesus Christ.

Concurrently with this new perspective, the Lord allowed me to start a new church in Dallas, Texas. This gave me an opportunity to emphasize in my preaching and teaching not gifts but maturity, both corporately and personally. On the one hand, I emphasized faith, hope, and love as reflections of *"Body* maturity." On the other hand, I emphasized the qualities for personal maturity specified in 1 Timothy 3 and Titus 1. And not surprisingly, in view of what the Bible emphasizes, I began to see more body function take place than at any other time in my ministry—and without confusion, rationalization, and self-deception.

Practical Steps for Developing Body Function in Your Church

The following project is designed to help you to become a more effective functioning member of Christ's body. It is also designed to help other Christians do the same.

Step 1

Note that most biblical references to the functioning body of Christ focus on local churches. The exceptions appear in some of Paul's statements in the Ephesian and Colossian letters. Even here, it must be recognized that believers can only function practically and minister to each other in close relationships. For example, I realize that I am a vital part of the universal body of Christ wherever it is located, but I cannot "hurt" or "rejoice" with someone that I do not know exists.

People suffering for Christ in China are unknown to me. Therefore, I have difficulty hurting with them. But I can identify with suffering saints in drought-ridden North Africa or in the Oklahoma dust bowls because we know the reality of such extended hot, dry spells in Texas.

The only possible way for body function to be effective, meaningful, and dynamic is in the context of local bodies of believers who know each other well and who are able, on the basis of that knowledge, to minister to each other. They are indeed part of the universal body of Christ. They represent local manifestations of the universal body. In these local manifestations true body function takes place.

Step 2

It's important to understand a local body of believers does not function automatically. There must be a degree of spiritual maturity. In order to become mature, believers must be taught the nature of the body of Christ. This, of course, is why Paul took so much effort to spell this out in the Corinthian letter.

Interestingly, when Paul wrote to the Ephesian and Colossian Christians, he nowhere described the nature of the human body. He talked directly about the functioning body of Christ, assuming understanding, insight, and perception. This is not surprising when you compare the maturity level of the groups. The Ephesians and Colossians were much further along in their spiritual development.

Note Paul's direct references to the functioning body of Christ in these letters:

- "And God . . . appointed Him [Jesus] to be head over everything for the church, which is *His body*" (Eph. 1:22-23).

- "His [Christ's] purpose was to create in Himself one new man out of the two [Jews and Gentiles], thus making peace, and in this *one body* to reconcile both of them to God through the cross" (Eph. 2:15-16).
- "There is *one body* and one Spirit" (Eph. 4:4).
- "It was He who gave some . . . to prepare God's people for works of service, so that the *body of Christ* may be built up" (Eph. 4:11-12).
- "From Him [Christ] the *whole body*, joined and held together by every supporting ligament, grows and builds itself up in love, as each part does its work" (Eph. 4:16).
- "For the husband is the head of the wife as Christ is the head of the church, *His body*" (Eph. 5:23).
- "For we are members of His [Christ's] *body*" (Eph. 5:30).
- "And He [Christ] is the head of the *body*, the church" (Col. 1:18).
- "I [Paul] fill up in my flesh what is still lacking in regard to Christ's afflictions for the sake of His *body,* which is the church" (Col. 1:24).
- "He [an unspiritual person] has lost connection with the Head, from whom the *whole body*, supported and held together by its ligaments and sinews, grows as God causes it to grow" (Col. 2:19).

Step 3

Either as a Christian leader or as a regular member of Christ's body, are you emphasizing "looking for gifts" or are you emphasizing "becoming spiritually mature"? Emphasizing looking for gifts can lead to confusion, rationalization, and even self-deception. An emphasis on becoming spiritually mature will lead to concern, humility, patience, sensitivity, freedom, and unity. These are true expressions of love.

Step 4

If you are a pastor (or in another position of Christian leadership), what are you doing to help other Christians become participating members of Christ's body? Check yourself!

——— I'm doing all I can to help other believers become mature in Christ—measured according to the qualities specified in 1 Timothy 3 and Titus 1.[1]

——— I look for as many opportunities as possible to encourage other mature Christians to participate in teaching the Scriptures, praying, helping others, counseling, etc.

——— I realize that God can use other members of the body of Christ, even though they may not have had as much training as I have.

——— I have a subtle sense of pride which keeps telling me I'm the only one capable of effectively ministering to other people.

——— I have difficulty trusting other members of Christ's body—either because I have not viewed other Christians properly, or I am threatened by the fact that they might be able to do things better than I can.

Isolate your areas of strength and weakness, and then *accentuate* your strengths and work at *eliminating* your weaknesses. Set up specific goals, including contact with specific individuals in your church.

Note: To start, select one person you are going to help become a more functioning member of Christ's body.

---

[1] For a helpful study of these qualities of maturity, see Gene A. Getz, *The Measure of a Man* (Glendale, Calif.: Regal Books, 1974).

2

Devoted to One Another

"*Be devoted to one another* in brotherly love" (Rom.
12:10, NASB).

I had the privilege of being the firstborn child of wonderful
parents. As years passed, I was followed by three brothers
and two sisters (actually three girls, but my sister Joann died
at age three).

Dad and Mom are salt-of-the-earth people. They've been
farmers all their lives (now retired). They never had much
education (Dad finished the sixth grade; Mom the eighth),
but they learned most of what they needed to know in the
school of experience. They, like most people their age, weath-
ered the Depression and were able to keep us fed and clothed.
We never lacked the important things in life—but neither did
we have many luxuries.

We had the usual problems of growing up, of course. But
we were basically a close-knit family. Sure, as kids we had our
knock-down drag-outs, and we all went through the usual
selfish stages that all kids go through. But I distinctly remember, as the oldest, that "fighting with each other" was

our privilege—no one else's. Let no one else lay a hand on my brothers and sisters! I was ready to defend them.

And Mom and Dad? They made mistakes; they were far from perfect. But they were *our* parents. They loved us and cared for us. They were devoted to us even when we were anything but appreciative and cooperative. And their greatest contribution to us was our spiritual heritage—the knowledge that we could become a part of the family of God.

Today, all the children are grown. Dad and Mom are growing old. But we're more devoted to each other now than ever before. Some of us don't see each other very often because we're miles apart. But when we get together, it's a great time, especially as we reflect on childhood experiences and God's grace in allowing us to be a family unit.

The Family of God

Being a part of a family is something with which most people can identify. This is why Paul wrote what he did in Romans 12:10. With the exhortation to "be devoted to one another in brotherly love," he introduced the Roman Christians (and us) to another analogy to illustrate the functioning church. He was referring to the *family unit.*

The "body" concept graphically portrays that Christians are "members one of another." Each believer (no matter what his or her status in life) is necessary and vitally important in God's order of things. The "family" concept gives us an even greater appreciation of what a functioning church should be. The "human body" serves as a beautiful illustration, but as with all analogies, it can go only so far in describing reality. Its more significant contribution is to illustrate *how* the church functions.

The concept of the family adds a dimension of warmth, tenderness, concern, and loyalty—in short, human emotion and devotion. Put another way, in using the "body" analogy,

Paul drew upon the physical aspects in the illustration to emphasize the necessity of every member's participation in the church. But when he used the "family" analogy, he was illustrating the psychological aspects of relational Christianity.

"Be Devoted to One Another *in Brotherly Love*"

The term "brotherly love" (*philadelphia*) refers to the love that should exist between brothers and sisters within family units. Applied to the functioning church, it refers to the love Christians should have for each other as brothers and sisters in Christ. We are also a family—the family of God! Paul acknowledged this when he prayed for the Ephesian Christians: "For this reason I kneel before the Father, from whom the whole *family of* believers in heaven and on earth derives its name" (Eph. 3:14; see also 1 Peter 4:17).

The term "brothers" (*adelphos*) is used to refer to the "Christian family" approximately 230 times, throughout the New Testament, beginning in the Book of Acts. The term is not exclusively used by Paul, but also by the other New Testament writers. Luke, James, and John use the term on the average as many times as Paul.[1]

The word *brother*s literally means "from the same womb." It is distinctly a "family term." When it refers to Christians, it means "fellow believers," "members of God's family," "brothers and sisters in Christ." It means we have all been "born again" into God's forever family. We are vitally related to each other through a common heritage. "In love He predestined us to be *adopted as sons* through Jesus Christ" (Eph. 1:5).

---

[1] Following is the approximate number of times the term "brother" or "brothers" is used in the New Testament, beginning in the Book of Acts: Acts (43); Romans (19); 1 Corinthians (37); 2 Corinthians (12); Galatians (10); Ephesians (3); Philippians (9); Colossians (5); 1 Thessalonians (19); 2 Thessalonians (9); 1 Timothy (3); 2 Timothy (1); Philemon (4); Hebrews (10); James (18); 1 Peter (11); 2 Peter (2); 1 John (17); 3 John (3); Revelation (5).

"Be Devoted to One Another in Brotherly Love"

Paul's use of the words, "be devoted to one another," enhances and supports his emphasis on brotherly love and family relationships in the church. To "be devoted" literally refers to the mutual love of parents and children and husbands and wives. It could be translated "show loving affection" or "love tenderly." Thus the King James Version reads: "Be *kindly affectioned* one to another with brotherly love." And Beck translates: "*Love one another tenderly* as fellow Christians."

Paul's point is clear. Christians are to be just as devoted to each other as are the individual members of a close-knit family unit. For we *are* a unique family unit. We are indeed "blood brothers," for in Christ "we have redemption through His blood, the forgiveness of sins" (Eph. 1:7).

We all remember the story of Tom Sawyer and Huckleberry Finn. These two young adventurers signed a pact with their own blood, committing themselves to one another. Blood brothers would do anything for one another—even die for one another!

Christians begin as infants—babes—in Christ. We go through various stages of development. In our immaturity we can easily fall into patterns of self-centered behavior. But as we mature, our lives should reflect the nature of Christ. This is why Paul exhorted the members of "the Philippian family" to "do nothing out of selfish ambition or vain conceit, but in humility consider others better than yourselves. Each of you should look not only to your own interests, but also to the interests of others" (Phil. 2:3-4).

Practical Steps for Developing Family Relationships in Your Church

Step 1

Showing affection and love to other Christians and treating them as brothers and sisters in Christ does not happen automatically. If it were automatic, we would not have so many exhortations to do so. Our first step must be to take seriously what the Bible says about brotherly love. Study carefully the following additional exhortations. Ask God to help you take them seriously as being a necessary part of walking in His will:

- "Now about *brotherly love* we do not need to write to you, for you yourselves have been taught by God to love each other. And in fact, you do love all the brothers throughout Macedonia. Yet we urge you, *brothers,* to do so *more and more*" (1 Thes. 4:9-10).

- "Keep on loving each other as brothers. Do not forget to entertain strangers, for by so doing some people have entertained angels without knowing it. Remember those in prison as if you were their fellow prisoners, and those who are mistreated as if you yourselves were suffering" (Heb. 13:1-3).

- "Now that you have purified yourselves by obeying the truth so that you have *sincere love for your brothers,* love one another deeply, with all your hearts. For you have been born again, not of perishable seed, but of imperishable, through the living and enduring Word of God" (1 Peter 1:22-23).

- "Finally, all of you, live in harmony with one another; be sympathetic, *love as brothers,* be compassionate and humble. Do not repay evil with evil or insult with insult, but with blessing, because to this you were called so that you may inherit a blessing" (1 Peter 3:8-9).

- "For this very reason, make every effort to add to your faith goodness; and to goodness, knowledge; and to knowledge, self-control; and to self-control, perseverance; and to perseverance, godliness; and to godliness, *brotherly kindness;* and to *brotherly kindness,* love" (2 Peter 1:5-7).

Step 2

Evaluate your attitudes and actions toward other members of your "Christian family." To what extent do you experience emotion and affection toward each fellow Christian? Note that Paul, in the context in which he exhorted Christians to "be devoted to one another in brotherly love," also exhorted that we "rejoice with those who rejoice" and "mourn with those who mourn" (Rom. 12:15). This, of course, involves *emotion: deep feelings* of joy as well as deep feelings of sadness.

Some Christians find it difficult to identify with other believers at the "feeling" level. There are reasons for this. And every Christian who finds it difficult to express emotion toward others should examine his life carefully, seeking to break the "log jam" that holds him back.

Consider the following questions:

1. *Do I fear rejection?* Some individuals have been so deeply hurt by others they are afraid to express their feelings. They are not willing to take a chance of being hurt again.

This, of course, is no excuse for not reaching out to others. We must work towards a mature perspective on human relationships. Christians must be vulnerable. And furthermore, most Christians to whom we reach out will not let us down. Don't let a bad experience rob you of God's best. Act on what you know to be the right thing to do.

Nancy had been rejected by her father. Nothing she did seemed to please him, especially when she couldn't maintain a B average in high school. She withdrew from making further attempts to win his approval. This attitude carried over into her adult life. She seemed continually withdrawn. She couldn't risk the chance of being rejected again, so she never attempted those creative activities which would win recognition.

2. *Have I had a poor family background?* Some people grow up in homes where physical affection and love toward

other family members are seldom or perhaps never expressed. For example, Mary grew up in a home where there was little affection demonstrated among family members. This does not mean they didn't love each other. They just didn't demonstrate it outwardly or with emotion. Her husband Bill's experience was just the opposite. Consequently, he has always found it easy to physically express affection to others. Mary, however, had to learn this process as an adult—which was often difficult, but she has done well. But, of course, it took time.

When people have been taught by example and practice to keep their feelings inside and to never express them, this attitude usually carries over in dealing with members of the family of God. It takes time to reverse such behavioral patterns.

Note: Some Christians also have difficulty expressing emotions to God because of negative experiences in the home—particularly with an earthly father. These emotions are very easily transferred to the "heavenly Father"—as well as to other members of the body of Christ.

If this explanation represents your situation, seek help from a fellow Christian you trust—someone who will not condemn you but will listen to you with sympathy and concern. Share your deepest and innermost feelings. Pray together.

A second note: Some people who have been severely repressed in childhood, and who have experienced unusual trauma, may need professional counsel. This kind of problem is not so much spiritual, but psychological in its roots.

3. *Am I basically angry and resentful?* Some Christians are controlled by deep feelings of anger and resentment toward other people. They are usually individuals who have repressed these feelings in early childhood. They find it very difficult to express positive emotions even toward fellow Christians.

4. *Do I spend most of my time thinking about myself?* Some Christians are very selfish and self-centered. They think only about themselves. They could care less about their brothers and sisters in Christ. Naturally, they find it difficult to express "brotherly love."

This selfish attitude is often expressed in prayers. Larry discovered how often he pleaded with God to give him things. Almost every prayer centered in Larry's desires for himself. Fortunately he noticed how others in the church spent considerable time praying for those with greater needs. He decided to put others on the top of his prayer list. Life soon took on new meaning.

Step 3

If you identify with any of the above, seek help from a fellow member of the body of Christ who is mature, someone you trust. Whatever step you take, begin to act immediately on what you know to be God's will. For example, if you have difficulty telling a fellow Christian you love him, force yourself to act on what you know is the right thing to do. Start by sharing with that person a gift, a note of appreciation, an invitation to dinner. Frequently, feelings begin to follow actions—particularly when you are emotionally rewarded and appreciated for your acts of kindness. Expressing love in a tangible way will help you to eventually develop feelings of love which you can share verbally.

Note: If you've been deeply hurt and. frustrated or repressed, don't allow yourself to withdraw. You'll only become more disillusioned. Your problems will get worse. Most people interpret one with reserved behavior as someone who needs little love or attention. Worse yet, they look upon such a person as someone who really doesn't want to be involved with other people. One quickly becomes isolated from those who could offer the greatest help.

THE FAMILY OF GOD

CHORUS:

I'm so glad I'm a part of the family of God;
I've been washed in the fountain, cleansed by the blood;
Joint heirs with Jesus as we travel this sod,
For I'm part of the family, the family of God.
You will notice we say brother and sister 'round here—
It's because we're a family and these folks are so dear.
When one has a heartache we all share the tears
And rejoice in each vict'ry in this family so dear.

From the door of an orph'nage to the house of the king,
No longer an outcast, a new song I sing.
From rags unto riches, from the weak to the strong,
I'm not worthy to be here, but praise God, I belong.

3

Honor One Another

"Honor one another above yourselves" (Rom. 12:10).

I have a Christian friend I especially admire because of a particular quality in his life. He's a musician—a pianist extraordinary. I'm not exaggerating when I say he can hold his own with the best Christian pianists in the country. He has perfect tonal memory. His creativity at the keyboard is amazing—at least to an amateur like me.

Yes, I admire his musicianship! But that's not what I had in mind when I began this chapter. What I admire the most is this man's desire to help other people "look and sound good"—especially when he accompanies them.

I've watched this happen and it's exciting. He always makes sure his own volume is "just right" so as not to compete with the vocalist. His "frills and ripples"—which flow from his fingers beautifully and naturally—always enhance the other's presentation rather than detract from it. He is able to accentuate when necessary to assist the singer in hitting difficult notes—or to even cover up a person's mistakes. What's most important, his excitement and personal satisfaction is always obvious when a vocalist he has accompanied is honored by others for a job well done.

When reflecting on Paul's injunction to "honor one another above ourselves," I could not help but think of my friend. To me, he is an excellent example—not only to other Christian musicians, but to all members of Christ's family. Every Christian should strive to make other believers "look and sound good." Every Christian should rejoice when others achieve, when others are honored, when others are successful. When this happens, the body of Christ will function beautifully and mature and grow in Christ.

Christ's Supreme Example

Jesus Christ, when He walked among men, set the supreme example in honoring others above Himself. On one occasion, a short time before His death, He taught the disciples a powerful truth. At an evening meal together, Jesus—knowing full well "that the Father had put all things under His power, and that He had come from God and was returning to God"— filled a basin with water and stooped to wash His disciples' feet. After He had finished the task, He shared with them a lesson I'm sure they never forgot.

"Do you understand," He asked, "what I have done for you?" Then He went on to answer His own question. "You call me 'Teacher' and 'Lord,' and rightly so, for that is what I am. Now that I, your Lord and Teacher, have washed your feet, you also should wash one another's feet. I have set you *an example* that you should do as I have done for you" (John 13:12-15).

It's my opinion that some Christians confuse principle and practice in this story, and to this very day they engage in "foot washing." I certainly respect their desire to be obedient to Christ and admire them for their actions. There is certainly freedom in Christ for us to practice this ancient custom today.

But I believe Jesus Christ wanted us to learn the *principle*. Though cultures change, though modes of transportation have evolved, and though we usually walk on sidewalks with shoes on our feet—one thing has not changed! Paul confirmed this when he said that we as Christians are to "honor one another above ourselves." This, it seems, is what Jesus was illustrating in the foot-washing episode.

On another occasion Jesus spelled this truth out even more clearly. He took the religious leaders to task for their pride and arrogance. "Everything they do is done for men to see," He said. "They love the place of honor at banquets and the most important seats in the synagogues; they love to be greeted in the marketplaces and have men call them 'Rabbi.' "

Then Jesus turned to His disciples and drove home the lesson they had to learn if they were to be mature men of God who could be used in His service: "The greatest among you will be your servant. For whoever exalts himself will be humbled, and whoever humbles himself will be exalted" (Matt. 23:5-12).

Paul's Dynamic Application

The Apostle Paul, though he never sat at the feet of Christ while He taught on earth, nevertheless learned this lesson well. He also applied this truth in his ministry to the New Testament churches. Thus he wrote to the Philippians: "Your attitude should be the same as that of Christ Jesus" (Phil. 2:5).

What was that attitude? Paul carefully spelled it out! Christ demonstrated towards all mankind the greatest act of unselfishness, humility, and self-sacrifice ever known in the universe: "Who, being in very nature God, did not consider equality with God something to be grasped, but made Himself nothing, taking the very nature of a servant, being made in human likeness. And being found in the appearance as a man, He humbled Himself and became obedient to death—even death on a cross!" (Phil. 2:6-8)

The result of Christ's act of love and submission brought to Himself in essence the very same result He promised His disciples if they would "honor others above themselves"—exaltation! This is what God did for Jesus Christ: "Therefore God exalted Him to the highest place and gave Him the name that is above every name, that at the name of Jesus every knee should bow, in heaven and on earth and under the earth, and every tongue confess that Jesus Christ is Lord, to the glory of God the Father" (Phil. 2:9-11).

Our personal exaltation, of course, is different. And it always will be different from that of Christ's. Nevertheless, God *will* exalt Christians who truly honor others above themselves. It may not be immediate, but it will happen. If not on earth, throughout all eternity where it will really count.

Yes, Paul understood this principle and applied it without equivocation. To make sure the Philippians understood what he meant by imitating Christ's attitudes and actions, he introduced the paragraph about Christ's act of humility and unselfishness by saying: "Do nothing out of selfish ambition or vain conceit, but *in humility consider others better than yourselves*. Each of you should look not only to your own interests, but also to the interests of others" (Phil. 2:3-4).

Practical Steps for Applying This Principle Today
Step 1

To evaluate your attitudes toward other Christians, the following questions will help pinpoint your strengths and weaknesses:

How many situations can you recall where you purposely attempted to honor someone above yourself? In what ways did you reflect *sincere* appreciation for the other person?

Note: Some people use this technique as a selfish device, knowing that promoting someone else will bring self-promotion. Bill is that kind of person. Some call him a "back-slapper." His unverbalized motto is: "I'll scratch your back if you'll scratch mine." He lives by a revised "golden rule": "Do unto others so they will do for you."

This kind of tactic usually is discernible. Furthermore, it usually backfires. It doesn't ring true. It contains elements of insincerity. If results are not immediate, the person with wrong motives often becomes impatient and reverses his field. Sometimes he will "put people down" whom he previously built up. This is flattery and sinful behavior. Beware if this is your temptation!

Observation: If you cannot easily recall several situations in which you have attempted to carry out Paul's injunction, you are probably not "honoring others above yourself."

Step 2

If it is difficult for you to compliment others and enjoy their successes, take a close look at your personality. Why is this true? The following checkpoints will help:

1. Some people cannot compliment others and enjoy their success because they have always been the center of attention themselves. They want *all* the attention.

Jane was an only child and had always had everything she wanted. Over the years she has become a self-centered and selfish person. Now as an adult, she finds it very difficult to even compliment her husband. Rather, she tends to "compete" with him. Unfortunately, her problem is about to destroy her marriage.

This, of course, represents a serious spiritual and emotional problem and reflects immaturity and carnality. This was the problem with the Corinthians. If this is your problem, confess your sin and re-program your life. Memorize Philippians 2:3-4, and meditate on it every day.

Every time you're tempted to "hog the show," quote these verses to yourself. Ask God to bring them to your memory when you find yourself being tempted.

2. There is another category of Christians who have difficulty complimenting and honoring others. The results are the same, but the emotional dynamics are different. These people, rather than being purely self-centered, are usually very insecure. They have difficulty "honoring others" because they feel in need of honor themselves. In fact, they are the kind of people who can never get enough honor and attention. They feed on it; they gorge themselves—and still cry out for more! Even after all this they often complain no one pays attention to them.

Tom is that kind of person. As a child he was always "put down." His parents were so busy trying to get attention from each other they failed to give any to Tom. Consequently, he grew up an insecure person. Now he finds within himself an insatiable desire for recognition and attention.

And he'll do almost anything to get it.

This represents a psychological problem as well as a spiritual one. Somewhere in their past, people like Tom were never given enough love and attention. Consequently, they developed a sponge-like personality. They cannot give; they must always receive.

A person of this kind needs insight, understanding, and help from others. He needs to recognize the necessity of reprogramming his mind and emotions. In addition to memorizing Scripture (such as Philippians 2:3-4), he needs loving counsel blended with direct confrontation regarding his patterns of behavior.

If you identify with this problem, begin today to seek help from another mature member of Christ's church. Don't disobey God another day (no matter what the cause of your problem). If you continue, you'll rob yourself of the blessing that will come if you truly "honor others above yourself."

Remember, you can never lose by sincerely honoring others. God will not forget, and neither will those you honor.

ETERNAL LIFE

Lord, make me an instrument of your peace,
    Where there is hatred, let me sow love—
    Where there is injury, pardon—
    Where there is doubt, faith—
    Where there is despair, hope—
    Where there is darkness, light—
    Where there is sadness, joy.

O Divine Master, grant that I may not so much seek
    To be consoled—as to console,
    To be understood—as to understand,
    To be loved—as to love,

For
    It is in giving that we receive,
    It is in pardoning that we are pardoned,
    It is in dying that we are born to eternal life.

        St. Francis of Assisi

4

Be of the Same Mind with One Another

"Now may the God who gives perseverance and encouragement grant you to *be of the same mind with one another* according to Christ Jesus" (Rom. 15:5, NASB).

There is one outstanding lesson we can learn from church history: Satan's primary strategy involves destroying unity among Christians. He is the author of confusion, insensitivity, false doctrine, and church splits. Turning to the Bible, one soon discovers the power whereby Satan's strategy can be defeated. It's the power of "one-mindedness" in the body of Christ.

Christ's Prayer for Unity
In Christ's prayer to the Father in John 17, He made direct reference to at least four major elements in the incomparable message of Christianity—*salvation* (17:1b-3); *incarnation* (17:4-6); *sanctification* (17:17-19); and *glorification* (17:24). Central in this beautiful and profound prayer is one major request—that His disciples (and Christians of all time) might experience unity and oneness. "Holy Father," prayed Jesus, "protect them by the power of Your name—the name

36

You gave Me—so that they may be *one* as we are one" (John 17:11).

Later, Jesus amplified this request: "My prayer is not for them alone. I pray also for those who will believe in Me through their message, *that all of them may be one*, Father, just as You are in Me and I am in You. May they also be in us so that the world may believe that You have sent Me. I have given them the glory that You gave Me, that they may be *one* as We are one; I in them and You in Me. May they be brought to complete *unity* to let the world know that You sent Me and have loved them even as You have loved Me." (John 17:20-23).

Jesus Christ's primary concern for His church stands out boldly in this prayer. It is a visible *unity*—a *oneness*—that reveals the very essence of the Christian Gospel. And that essence comprises the fact "that God was reconciling the world to Himself in Christ" (2 Cor. 5:19). Jesus Christ was indeed God in the flesh. He was (and is) one with the Father. And oneness in Christ's body in some miraculous and marvelous way reveals to men who observe that unity that Christ was indeed God. If He had not been God, there could have been no plan of salvation. Christianity would be just another man-made religion.

Earlier I mentioned that Satan's strategy throughout church history has been to destroy unity in Christ's body. This makes a lot of sense from Satan's point of view. If he can destroy unity, he has destroyed the most powerful means of communication to lost men that Jesus Christ was God. When that message is obliterated or even blurred, man is doomed to eternal despair. Man cannot come to know God apart from coming to know Jesus Christ who was the Son of God (John 20:30-31).

When Christ was on earth, He worked miracles to convince men He was God. When He went back to heaven, He left His church to communicate that truth. And the ingredient in the church that convinces non-Christians that Jesus was God is *unity*—being of "the same mind with one another." This, too, represents a miracle because men everywhere tend toward disunity. History flows with lack of harmony among mankind. Wars have been the norm—the standard for human behavior. And when non-Christians see true unity and true oneness, their hearts cry out to be a part of that kind of love.

It was no accident, of course, that Jesus, when praying that His followers might be one, also made this request: "My prayer is not that You take them out of this world but that You *protect them from the evil one*" (John 17:15). Jesus knew in advance that Satan's tactic would be to destroy unity in the body of Christ. Thus He prayed that God would protect believers from those things that destroy oneness while they fulfilled God's purpose on earth.

The Jerusalem Church—A Dynamic Example

Immediately following Christ's return to heaven, the church in Jerusalem emerged as a direct answer to Jesus' prayer. Their unity was profound. Luke records, "And day by day continuing *with one mind* in the temple, and breaking bread from house to house, they were taking their meals together with gladness and sincerity of heart" (Acts 2:46, NASB). And later Luke adds, *"All* the believers were *one in heart and mind"* (Acts 4:32).

This does not mean that there were no problems, that Satan did not try to destroy their unity. Luke records that certain widows were being neglected in the daily distribution of food. This created unhappiness and complaints—in short, lack of unity. But the apostles, facing the problem with wisdom and discretion, appointed qualified men to handle the situation. The problem was soon solved. Once again unity was restored. (See Acts 6:1-4.)

What is more significant than these *accounts* of unity are the *results* of that unity. These appear again as a direct answer to Christ's high priestly prayer in John 17. His prayer was that unity might reveal the fact that He had come in the flesh to save all men from their sins. In Acts 2, following Luke's report of unity in the Jerusalem church, we read that they enjoyed "the favor of *all the people*"—obviously the non-Christians in Jerusalem. We also read that "the Lord added to their number daily those who were *being saved*" (Acts 2:47).

Following Luke's account that "all the believers were one in heart and mind," we read: "With *great power* the apostles continued to testify to the resurrection of the Lord Jesus, and much grace was with them all" (Acts 4:32-33). Again we see a direct correlation between unity in the body of Christ and the result of that unity in the lives of non-Christians.

It should not surprise us, then, that we see the same pattern in Acts 6, following the restoration of unity that was interrupted by the needy widows. Once they had faced the problem and solved it, "the Word of God spread. The number of disciples in Jerusalem *increased rapidly*, and a large number of priests became obedient to the faith" (Acts 6:7).

Paul's Primary Concern

We've already noticed that Jesus' concern for unity in the church was also Paul's concern. Christ's prayer was also Paul's prayer: "May the God who gives endurance and encouragement give you a *spirit of unity* among yourselves as you follow Christ Jesus, so that with *one heart and mouth* you may glorify the God and Father of our Lord Jesus Christ" (Rom. 15:5-6).

Earlier in his Roman letter Paul had already exhorted: "Live *in harmony* with one another" (Rom. 12:16). And again: "Let us therefore make every effort to do what leads to *peace* and to mutual edification" (Rom. 14:19).

Paul gave the same basic exhortation to the Ephesian and Philippian Christians. To the Ephesians, he wrote: "Make every effort to keep the *unity of the Spirit* through the *bond of peace*" (Eph. 4:3). And to the Philippians, he said: "Whatever happens, conduct yourselves in a manner worthy of the Gospel of Christ. Then, whether I come and see you or only hear about you in my absence, I will know that you stand firm in *one spirit,* contending as *one man* for the faith of the Gospel" (Phil. 1:27).

We conclude that a functioning church must be a unified church. In fact, unity is a reciprocal dynamic. Unity creates effective body function; effective body function creates more unity. Where there is unity, there will be a dynamic witness for Jesus Christ. "Body visibility" that reflects oneness also reflects the heart of the Christian Gospel—that Jesus Christ is truly the God-Man. He was in God, and God was in Him. He was (and is) *one* with the Father.

Practical Steps for Developing Unity in Your Church
Step 1
Realize first that unity *is* possible. There is, of course, a spiritual unity that binds all believers together within the universal Church. Even those we do not know—and never will know till we are in heaven—are one with us in Christ. But the unity that Jesus and Paul prayed for is a concrete, visible, and practical unity that can exist among believers who are bound together in a particular geographical location. It is day-by-day, gut-level unity. It involves flesh and blood people in relationship with each other. This is what was obvious in Jerusalem.

Unity and oneness *is* possible, then, in a local church. Though many different personalities are part of any given local family of believers, yet they can be drawn together as one heart and one soul.

This is a great mystery, but it is possible in Jesus Christ. If it was the spiritual dynamic of many of the New Testament churches (and it was, even where slaves and slave owners sat side-by-side as brothers in Christ), then it can also be true of 20th-century churches who also "make every effort to keep the unity of the Spirit through the bond of peace" (Eph. 4:3).

Step 2

Realize that unity in a local church is not automatic. As Paul exhorted, it takes *effort*. True, there is positional unity —because we are in Christ. But the practical and visible unity comes when every believer does his part.

Imagine what would have happened to the unity in the Jerusalem church if the apostles had not faced the reality of the neglected widows. No doubt it would have resulted in the first major local church split.

Imagine what would have happened if the leaders in Antioch had not faced the theological problem created by the Judaizers (Acts 15). If they hadn't solved the problem with the help of the Jerusalem council, it may have resulted in theological confusion and division all over the New Testament world. But because they faced the problem and did something about it, unity was restored.

All of this says that maintaining unity is two-dimensional. First, Christ prayed (and is praying) for us. We have supernatural help available to defeat Satan. Second, we must "make every effort" to see that we do not allow human factors to create irritations to bring about misunderstandings which divide us. Satan delights in using trivia to destroy local churches.

In one church, two men had made pledges to purchase a new organ. Rather than pledging in a general way to an organ fund, each man specified the brand of organ to which his large donation would apply. Friends of each man sided with their particular friend. They argued among themselves. Some even left the church. Ironically, the church never bought either organ. The only winner in the situation—Satan!

Step 3
Realize that the key to unity is Christian maturity, reflecting love. This, of course, is what the previous chapter is all about. And this is best illustrated (in a negative fashion) by the Corinthian church. They were woefully immature and unloving in their attitudes and actions. Consequently, they represent the most carnal, divisive, and disunified church in the whole New Testament world.

Step 4
The next chapter deals with the practical aspects for creating unity. Read it carefully and evaluate your own efforts at creating oneness in Christ's body.

5

Accept One Another

"Accept one another, then, just as Christ accepted you, in order to bring praise to God" (Rom. 15:7).

I grew up in a church where "acceptance" by others depended primarily on what you did or did not do. And, as you might guess, the list of "do's and don'ts" certainly did not comprise a *biblical* list. Rather, it consisted of extra-scriptural activities, most of which were cultural.

What I'm describing, of course, is 20th-century legalism. And nothing shatters true unity among Christians more thoroughly than extra-biblical rules and regulations which are used to evaluate a person's relationship with Jesus Christ. When acceptance or rejection of others is based on a legalistic mind-set, it leads rapidly to judgmental behavior and pseudo-spirituality. It also creates false guilt, destroys personal freedom to really be what God wants a Christian to be, and often leads to a violation of the true biblical standards for Christian behavior.

A lot of wonderful people attended the church in which I grew up, and there was a certain loyalty within the group, yet little spiritual unity or in-depth spirituality was exhibited. Those who became part of the group were accepted only as they fulfilled a predetermined set of behavioral expectations. This legalism caused a great deal of false guilt, a problem I personally faced for years, till I understood what true spirituality is.

This is a sad commentary on what Christianity has come to be in many situations. The Bible does lay down behavioral expectations for Christians, but it also condemns acceptance or rejection based on external patterns that go beyond specific scriptural statements.

Paul deals with this subject clearly in his letter to the Romans. In fact, he presents acceptance of fellow Christians as a basic key to unity. Note the context of this injunction:

"May the God who gives endurance and encouragement give you a *spirit of unity* among yourselves as you follow Christ Jesus, so that with *one heart and mouth* you may glorify the God and Father of our Lord Jesus Christ. *Accept one another,* then, just as Christ *accepted you*" (Rom. 15:5–7).

In at least two areas Christians have historically violated the injunction "accept one another" by judging one another (legalism) and in showing partiality (prejudice). Interestingly, these problems go all the way back to New Testament churches. And the Bible speaks forcefully to both issues, condemning each as sin.

Judging One Another

To sit in false judgment on other Christians is a violation of Paul's exhortation to accept one another. Interestingly, he uses the two concepts concurrently to make his point in his Roman letter. Thus he wrote: "*Accept him* whose faith is weak, *without passing judgment* on disputable matters" (Rom. 14:1).

In this particular New Testament church (and others like it) some Christians had personal problems even while engaging in certain legitimate activities. These problems arose out of previous sinful associations with those activities. Others, however, were free from this very *real*, but false guilt.

In both the Roman and Corinthian churches, one of these activities involved eating meat that had been offered to idols. Paul, in his inimitable way, brought the problem into clear focus, particularly in his Corinthian letter: "So then, about eating meat sacrificed to idols: We know that an idol is nothing at all in the world, that there is no God but one. . . . But not everyone knows this. Some people are still so accustomed to idols that when they eat such meat, they think of it as having been sacrificed to an idol, and since their conscience is weak, it is defiled. But food does not bring us near to God; we are no worse if we do not eat, and no better if we do" (1 Cor. 8:4, 7-8; see also Rom. 14:14).

How did Paul deal with this problem? First, he spoke to both the weak and the strong: "The man who *eats everything* must not look down on him who does not, and the man *who does not eat everything* must not condemn the man who does, *for God has accepted him*" (Rom. 14:3). In other words, we are not to judge each other in areas that are not specified as sin. "Each one," said Paul, "should be fully convinced in his own mind" (Rom. 14:5).

Second, Paul directed his comments primarily to the strong in faith—to those who could eat meat offered to idols without sinning: "All food is clean, but it is wrong for a man to eat anything that causes someone else to stumble. It is better not to eat meat or drink wine or to do anything else that will cause your brother to fall. . . . We *who are strong* ought to bear with the failings of the weak, and not to please ourselves" (Rom. 14:20-21; 15:1).

After exhorting both the immature and mature Christians

not to judge one another, Paul then laid a heavy burden on mature Christians. If we are truly mature, we will be sensitive toward our brothers and sisters in Christ who are not strong as we are. We will be careful to do nothing that would cause them to stumble and fall into sin. If these two attitudes are working concurrently in a local body of believers, unity will inevitably emerge. Those who are weak will soon become strong, and those who are strong will become even more mature.

Showing Partiality

Paul introduced this barrier to unity in his Roman letter even before dealing with legalism. "Live in harmony with one another," he wrote. "Don't be proud, but be willing to associate with people of low position. Don't be conceited" (Rom. 12:16).

James, of all the New Testament writers, dealt with this problem most extensively. And like Paul, he allowed no room for misinterpretation about the sin of prejudice. "My brothers," he wrote, "as believers in our glorious Lord Jesus Christ, *don't show favoritism*" (James 2:1).

In the churches to which James was writing, Christians had difficulty accepting everyone in the same way. Their particular problem involved the rich and the poor. When a man came into their assembly well dressed and obviously rich, they immediately gave him the best seat. But when a poor man came in, dressed in shabby clothes, they ushered him to a seat less prominent. When you do this, queried James, "have you not discriminated among yourselves and become judges of evil thoughts?" (James 2:4). To make sure they really got his point, James spelled out the answer to his own questions in unequivocal terms: *"If you show favoritism, you sin"* (James 2:9).

Prejudice, favoritism, and discrimination in the body of

Christ violate the law of God. Furthermore, they violate the very nature of the functioning body of Christ. We are *all* one. Every member is important—rich or poor, young or old, black or white, weak or strong! If we show favoritism, we also destroy the unity, harmony, and oneness in the body of Christ which Christ and Paul both prayed for and commanded.

It is startling how some evangelical, Bible-believing churches over the years have justified prejudice. Of course, we can make the Bible teach anything we want—and this is exactly what we're doing when we bar any sincere and practicing Christian from participating in a local church. We are sinning against both God and man when we do this.

**Practical Steps to Help Christians
in Your Church Accept One Another**
Step 1
It's important, first of all, to make sure you (and other Christians in your church) really understand what Paul was teaching in Romans 14. This passage is woefully misinterpreted and misapplied. First, Paul was teaching that neither the weak nor the strong are to judge one another. This is a two-way responsibility. In many 20th-century churches, the strong are expected to bear full responsibility. This, of course, is a violation of Paul's teaching.

Second, the strong Christian is to be careful not to cause a weaker brother or sister to fall into sin.

Here is where many of today's Christians terribly misunderstand and violate Paul's teaching. "Offense" or "stumbling" is defined by some, especially immature Christians, as making them "feel bad" if another Christian does something they don't like. This is *not* what Paul meant by causing "distress" or "grief" or making someone stumble. Rather, he made it clear that this is judging and should not be. What Paul meant by "causing someone to stumble" is to cause a fellow Christian to actually do something he cannot do with a clear conscience, thus causing him to sin against himself and the Lord. Just making him "feel bad" is not causing him to stumble. In fact, some immature Christians "feel bad" because of selfishness.

There is yet another misinterpretation and misapplication of Paul's teaching in Romans 14. Ironically, some Christians set up extra-biblical standards for themselves and then require that all other Christians measure up to those same standards in order to be spiritual. This, of course, is also judging others and is not accepting others as we should.

An example of this: A certain Bible-preaching pastor has always preached against long hair for men. His personal style is that of the World War II GI. This is his *cultural* standard for evaluating the length of "long" (see 1 Cor. 11:14). While insisting that "long" hair is strictly a mark of rebellion against authority, he is making the generalization that an attitude present when the trend began is still present. "Long" hair has become, however, an acceptable hairstyle to most people, just as it was in the days of the Pilgrim Fathers. This pastor will not allow any long-haired men to sing in his choir . . . nor will he welcome any such men into church membership. Long-haired men must first visit a barber shop. Then they'll be considered spiritual enough to participate.

Note: The Bible *does* teach that Christians are to break fellowship with other Christians who continually live in sin, but only after following a definite biblical procedure. Make sure, however, that the "sin" can be definitely defined in the Bible: immorality, lying, stealing, gossip, etc. In these cases, Christians are to take at least three steps to solve the problem. First, we are to exhort in love the persons involved considering ourselves lest we also be tempted. Second, if they don't respond to loving exhortation and continue sinning, then we are to ask them to discontinue fellowship with other Christians in the church for a period of time. Finally, if they still do not respond, we are to have nothing to do with them, actually treating them as if they were unbelievers.

My experience has been that when a proper biblical approach is taken to disciplining others in the church, you seldom have to go beyond the first step. Most people who know Jesus Christ personally respond to loving exhortation.[1]

Step 2

Evaluate your own attitudes and actions. Are you "accepting" or "rejecting" people upon your own standards—standards you have set up or accepted because of your own weak conscience? If you are, you are "judging" your brother. This Paul forbids in Romans 14.

Note: I believe a Christian organization can set up certain "institutional" standards that are extra-biblical, and yet not violate the teaching of Scripture. But the moment we begin to evaluate other Christians' spirituality on the basis of these standards, and begin to promote these standards as marks of Christian maturity, we violate the teachings of Scripture. We are using a false criterion for measuring spirituality.

Challenge: If we teach and practice the true biblical criteria for spirituality, we will usually find it unnecessary to set up standards in addition to Scripture. (For an interesting study of a profile of Christian maturity, see the qualifications listed by Paul in 1 Timothy 3 and Titus 1.)

Step 3

Evaluate your attitude toward other Christians concerning prejudice and favoritism. Can you truly accept all other be-

---

[1] For a rather detailed study of how to handle sin in the lives of other Christians, see chapter 9.

lievers as brothers and sisters in Christ? Is this actually happening in your church?

Note: The greatest sin committed by many American Christians is racial prejudice. In many white churches, black Christians have not been welcome. If they are, they are discriminated against as lower-class Christians. There is no other word for this behavior than James' word—he called it sin! Paul also used a couple of other words to describe it—pride and conceit (Rom. 12:16).

Step 4

Follow this three-point plan for overcoming any problem in your life that reflects legalism and prejudice:

1. Acknowledge it as sin (1 John 1:9).

2. Pinpoint the areas of your life where you need to change. Ask God to help you overcome your sins. Pray *specifically* about *specific* problems.

3. Take an action step. For a starter, select another member of Christ's body you have had difficulty accepting. Do something for that person that reflects true Christian love. For example, you might invite that person to your home for dinner.

Warning: Don't wait until you "feel" like changing or doing something about your sin. If you do, the feelings may never come. Christian love acts on what is the right thing to do.

Suggestion: If your church is permeated with legalistic behavior and/or prejudice, ask your pastor or some other leader in your church to read this chapter and to give you his opinion as to whether or not it is scriptural. If his reactions are negative, then graciously ask him to give you biblical reasons for his conclusions.

6

Admonish One Another

"And concerning you, my brethren, I myself also am convinced that you yourselves are full of goodness, filled with all knowledge, and able also to *admonish one another*" (Rom. 15:14, NASB).

Some of the most significant relationships I've developed over the years have resulted from experiences in which I've had to confront another Christian about his sin. It has never been an easy task (I dread it every time). Yet in the end it usually (not always) has been a very emotionally and spiritually rewarding task. Furthermore, it always provides me an opportunity for personal, psychological and spiritual growth. I inevitably end up evaluating my own Christian life-style and frequently discover I need to make some changes too.

There is no greater sign of love than to be willing to risk rejection and broken relationships with others. And if admonishment is done in the right spirit, with the right motive, using an appropriate method, the person who is not living a life worthy of the Gospel of Christ usually senses the risk you're taking. Though that person may have difficulty acknowledging it at that moment, down deep he really knows. Some day he will probably thank you for your love.

Admonishment—What Is It?

Translators use various words to describe Paul's injunction to the Roman Christians. As we've seen, the *New American Standard Bible* reads "admonish one another." Williams uses the phrase "counsel one another." Beck, the word "correct." And the *New International Version* reads: "I myself am convinced, my brothers, that you yourselves are ... *competent to instruct one another.*"

Actually, the word *noutheteo* doesn't refer to casual communication or normal-type teaching. It implies a definite exhortation, correction, and warning. In the Thessalonian letter, the translators of the *New International Version* use the word "warn" to describe Paul's admonishment to Christians who were idle and lazy (1 Thes. 5:14; they use the same word in Acts 20:31 and 1 Cor. 4:14).

The exhortation in Paul's Roman letter (as recorded at the beginning of this chapter) certainly constitutes an appropriate follow-through to his rather intensive instructions to these Christians to "stop passing judgment on one another" (Rom. 14:13). Like so many injunctions in Scripture, here is another divine balance unique in religious literature. This should not surprise us because it appears as just another evidence that the Scriptures are truly inspired by God and profitable for doctrine (2 Tim. 3:16).

On the surface, Paul's instruction to the Roman Christians to "admonish" or to "warn" one another may appear as a contradiction to what he has just emphasized. How can Christians carry out this injunction without "judging"? The answer is inherent in the text—and even more obvious from the total context of Scripture.

The Basis for Being Competent to Admonish

Paul complimented these Christians by letting them know he was thoroughly convinced that they were "competent to instruct [or admonish] one another." He spelled out why he felt this way:

1. They were "full of goodness." You are "competent," Paul said, because you "are full of goodness." Through this tribute Paul expressed his confidence in their basic spirituality, in their progress in Christian development, and in their righteous and upright lives. In other words, these Christians were able to "admonish one another" because they were, generally speaking, living holy, Christlike lives. In the words of Jesus Christ Himself, they were mature enough to make sure they removed the "plank" from their own eyes before they tried to remove the "speck of sawdust" from their brother's eye (Matt. 7:3-5).

Christians who are sensitive about their own walk with God are capable—and responsible—to admonish other Christians. They have earned the right to warn those who display characteristics that violate the direct teaching of Scripture. It is one of the most difficult exhortations to obey, but it is necessary for the body of Christ to mature and grow.

Admonishment, when done according to biblical guidelines, is not "judging others." One of the first guidelines was spelled out by Paul: make sure you are "full of goodness" yourself. Putting it another way, we must make sure we "clean up our own act" before we try to help someone else "clean up" his.

2. They were "complete in knowledge." The second requirement for being able to admonish others is an adequate knowledge of God's Word. Paul commended the Roman Christians for their maturity in this area.

Admonishment must be based upon God's specific will and ways—not on what we think other Christians should or should not be doing. We must be careful at this point. Many Christians tend to confuse absolutes and non-absolutes. If we exhort Christians in areas that are extra-biblical—areas that are not specifically spelled out in Scripture or specific things that involve cultural standards and practices—then we are in danger of imposing standards contrary to Scripture.

The difference sometimes represents a very fine line. For while engaging in an activity that is not specifically forbidden in Scripture, a Christian may also be doing something that *is* definitely forbidden in Scripture. For example, the Bible does not specifically forbid reading modern literature, but it certainly warns against exposing our minds to impure and unrighteous things (Phil. 4:8).

Most of us have been through periods in our lives when we attended churches which had rather rigid lists of do's and don'ts. These had developed over the past 40 to 50 years as responses to cultural and doctrinal changes. Some had definite scriptural basing. Others were simply activities which were rejected by church leaders, especially pastors. Eventually we had to learn for ourselves which were right and which were wrong. Only then could we rightfully admonish others.

Our basis for admonishment, then, must be definitely supported by Scripture. It requires a good knowledge of the Word of God to appropriately admonish. In fact, if we are not learning the Scriptures as we should, we ourselves are in need of admonishment (2 Tim. 2:15).

The Proper Process

Other scriptural examples and exhortations treating the concept of admonishment give us some helpful guidelines for actually carrying out this process.

1. Admonishment must be done with deep concern and love. Paul himself appears in Scripture as an unusual example. When he met with the Ephesian elders on his way to Jerusalem, he exhorted them to be on guard against false teachers. Then he reminded them of their previous relationship. "Remember," he said, "that for three years I never

stopped warning [admonishing] each of you night and day *with tears"* (Acts 20:31). There was no doubt in these men's minds that Paul loved them. Paul's tears were a reflection of his deep concern for these brothers in Christ. In no way could they interpret this process as judging.

2. Admonishment, to be effective, must frequently be personal. This does not mean that there should never be general admonishment. This Paul did himself when writing his letters to various bodies of believers. But note that he reminded the Ephesian elders that he had warned each of them (see also 1 Thes. 2:11).

When a particular Christian has a particular problem, some pastors exhort the whole church, hoping the person who is in need of the exhortation is listening. This can be a "cop-out"— a way to avoid personal confrontation. Furthermore, the person on the listening end knows what is happening and resents it. Far better to make such exhortation a private matter. The results will be more rewarding.

Note: The Bible does speak about "public rebuke," but only after personal confrontation and sufficient evidence of continual sin is given by two or three witnesses (Matt. 18:15-17; 1 Tim. 5:19).

3. Admonishment must be persistent if it is to be effective. Note again that Paul's admonishment to the Ephesians was "night and day" and for a period of "three years." Mutual exhortation must be continual. It cannot stop after a brief encounter. The Word of God is filled with a multitude of exhortations, warnings, and instructions. It takes a lot of time to communicate them all—and a lifetime to apply them.

4. Admonishment must be done with pure motives. Again Paul emerges as a supreme example. To the Corinthians he wrote: "I am not writing this to *shame* you, but to warn [admonish] you, as my dear children" (1 Cor. 4:14). We must do all we can to avoid embarrassing people—even those

who are guilty. This is why personal confrontation should precede public confrontation. If an erring brother or sister is admonished privately and in Christian love, the need for public admonishment is often eliminated.

5. Admonishment must be done with a proper goal. There should be only one basic objective when we admonish others: to help them become more mature in Jesus Christ. Thus Paul wrote to the Colossians: "We proclaim Him, counseling [admonishing] and teaching everyone with all wisdom, *so that we may present everyone perfect in Christ*. To this *end* I labor, struggling with all the energy He so powerfully works in me" (Col. 1:28-29).

6. Admonishment must be a natural outgrowth of proper body function. There are two types of admonishment—preventive and corrective. The Scriptures teach us we are to warn each other to "stay away from sin" (preventive counseling). Thus far we have emphasized primarily the corrective type. But preventive counseling should be consistent in the church as the body of Christ functions as a group. This is what Paul was referring to when he wrote to the Colossians: "Let the Word of Christ dwell in you richly as you *teach* and *counsel* [admonish] *one another* with all wisdom, and as you sing psalms, hymns and spiritual songs with gratitude in your hearts to God" (Col. 3:16).

Practical Steps for Helping Christians to Properly Admonish Each Other
Step 1
Every Christian must evaluate his own life before trying to admonish others. The following questions will serve as personal criteria:

1. Can I say my own life is "full of goodness"? That is, am I living a holy and righteous life before God? If I am deliberately violating Scripture, I am not in a position to ad-

monish others. I must first of all deal with sin in my own life before I am ready to try to deal with sin in someone else's life.

2. Do I really know what the Bible teaches about godly and righteous living? If I don't, I have incomplete knowledge. Again, I am not in a position to admonish others.

Note: This does not mean I must know everything there is to know about the Scriptures before I admonish others. However, I must make sure that I really know what the Bible teaches in a particular area before I proceed.

3. When I exhort or admonish another Christian (or Christians), do I do so, reflecting deep love and concern? Or do I come across with a harsh manner and appear to others as if I'm angry? Remember, a Christian who is "able to teach" others is "kind" and "not resentful." And "those who oppose him he must gently instruct" (2 Tim. 2:24-25).

4. When a Christian needs admonishment regarding specific sins, do I seek that person out in a private setting, rather than use a "pulpit tactic" that makes it appear I'm speaking to everyone? Do I use the crowd to cover up my speaking to *only one* person?

5. Am I persistent in my admonishment without being obnoxious and overbearing?

6. Do I admonish others—not to tear them down and embarrass them—but to build them up?

7. Do I admonish others for one basic purpose—to help them become complete and mature in Christ?

8. Does our church structure make it natural and easy for all members of Christ's body to be involved in "mutal exhortation"? Or is the church structured so that only "the preacher" is involved?

Note: Many meetings in churches are not designed for proper body function. There is no opportunity for corporate sharing and "body life." Everything is so tightly programmed and structured that spontaneous instruction and counseling by members of the body cannot take place. If this is true in your church, you need to carefully evaluate your structure and make appropriate changes.

Step 2

These questions apply in a specific way to Christian parents who are responsible to admonish their children regarding a proper Christian life-style. If you are a parent (or are planning to be one), re-read the above questions from the perspective of a parent. How do you measure up? Are you indeed qualified to admonish your children? If not, remember you cannot suddenly become a "non-parent." Your only choice is to become qualified.

The same applies to every member of Christ's body. Because we are not qualified to admonish others does not exempt us from the responsibility. Rather, we are responsible before God to become mature in Christ so we in turn can help others become mature in Christ.

A Word of Encouragement: Remember that the Roman Christians were not perfect, and there were problems in the church. Some people were weak, others were strong. Both the weak and the strong were judging one another. Otherwise, Paul would not have had to "admonish" them about this matter. But even with these weaknesses, Paul said: "And concerning you, my brethren, I myself also am convinced that you yourselves are full of goodness, filled with all knowledge, and able also to admonish one another" (Rom. 15:14, NASB).

Lord, Speak to Me

Lord, speak to me, that I may speak in living echoes of Thy tone;
As Thou hast sought, so let me seek Thy erring children lost and lone.

*O teach me, Lord, that I may teach the precious things Thou
dost impart;*
*And wing my words, that they may reach the hidden depth
of many a heart.*

*O fill me with Thy fullness, Lord, until my very heart o'er-
flow*
*In kindling tho't and glowing word, Thy love to tell, Thy
praise to show.*

*O use me, Lord, use even me, just as Thou wilt, and when
and where;*
*Until Thy blessed face I see, Thy rest, Thy joy, Thy glory
share.*

7

Greet One Another

"Greet Priscilla and Aquila . . . . Greet also the church that meets at their house. Greet my dear friend Epaenetus . . . . Greet Mary, who worked very hard for you. . . . Greet *one another* with a holy kiss. *All the churches* of Christ send greetings" (Rom. 16:3-6, 16).

These folks represent only a few people whom Paul greeted personally as he closed his letter to the Roman believers. In fact, he mentioned 26 people by name, and his exhortation to "greet one another with a holy kiss" represents only one of five such exhortations in the New Testament letters (see also 1 Cor. 16:20; 2 Cor. 13:12; 1 Thes. 5:26; 1 Peter 5:14).

Some Christians have puzzled over this injunction—particularly the "holy kiss." Others have resolved the problem by practicing it in various forms even in 20th-century America. I grew up in a church where each Sunday men would greet men and women would greet women with a "holy kiss." Knowing the lack of love in the church, I often wondered how "holy" the kiss really was.

Most Christians, however, simply dismiss this biblical exhortation as purely cultural. (I don't remember hearing a sermon preached on this particular text; nor do I remember it ever being seriously treated in my biblical studies in either undergraduate or graduate school.)

What did Paul and Peter mean? Do these five injunctions (four by the Apostle Paul and one by the Apostle Peter) have any relevance to Christians living in the 20th century? When an exhortation is repeated five times in the New Testament, Christians ought to consider it seriously before dismissing it as irrelevant.

This injunction seems to have both cultural and supracultural dimensions. On the one hand, to "greet one another" is normative. On the other hand, the form of that greeting varies. Put another way, Christians are always to sincerely greet one another as brothers and sisters in Christ. The way that greeting is expressed depends on what is appropriate and acceptable in a given culture.

The Cultural Aspect

In order to properly interpret scriptural exhortations, we must understand the difference between "absolutes" and "non-absolutes." For example, we are to "teach and counsel one another," but the Bible does not lock us into a particular form or structure for that process to take place. We are told to "preach the Word," but are not told specifically how. In these cases, teaching, preaching, and counseling are basic functions that take on various forms. In fact, it is impossible to have function without form. It is possible, however, to talk about the function without describing the form. This the Bible does frequently.

Christians make a serious mistake when they superimpose particular cultural forms on biblical functions and then make the forms absolute as well as the functions. For example, some pastors teach that the Bible presents one-way communication as an absolute pattern, exclusive of other forms. This is the way they define preaching. (They will, of course, have difficulty explaining why Peter allowed dialogue in his sermon [Acts 2].)

To do this is the same as insisting that preaching must always be from the pulpit, arranged with three points, and delivered with forceful voice. The fact is, the Bible says nothing about the first two factors, and probably implies "loud voices" in most cases because they didn't have amplifiers.

Don't misunderstand. The Bible doesn't teach that these things are wrong. The Bible leaves us free to develop the forms that are most appropriate in any given culture, to carry out a normative biblical function.

Understanding the scriptural difference between function and form, supra-cultural absolutes and cultural non-absolutes, helps solve many problems in biblical interpretation. With this in mind, the injunction to "greet one another with a holy kiss" also becomes an understandable concept—relevant in the first century as well as the twentieth. On the one hand, the injunction to "greet one another" *is* supra-cultural; on the other hand, the kiss represents a *form* of greeting very common in the first century. It is still common in some cultures today. We've all observed heads of state of Middle Eastern and Eastern European countries greeting one another with a kiss. Most noticeable are the outward demonstrations by Russian leaders when they visit outside their country. They usually hold their host officials by both arms and then give a kiss on either the right or both cheeks. Some call the embrace a "Russian bear hug." They seem especially demonstrative when greeting officials of nearby Eastern European countries.

Paul's and Peter's concern was that the kiss be a "holy" one—a sanctified one—an expression of true Christian love. It was to demonstrate that believers were truly brothers and sisters in Christ. It was no longer to be *just* a greeting—a routine gesture that reflected the social graces of that particular culture.

The Bible gives several examples of greeting others with a kiss: Judas and Christ (Matt. 26:48-49); the father and his prodigal son (Luke 15:20); the Ephesian elders and Paul (Acts 20:37). Not one of these illustrations gives a specific description of the form a kiss took. Luke gives us a slight clue when he describes the parting scene between the Ephesian elders and Paul in Miletus. "And they all wept sore, and *fell on Paul's neck,* and *kissed him*" (Acts 20:37, KJV). Yet, the description is not terribly specific. We can only speculate from what we're told. It probably involved kissing his neck or his cheek. This, of course, conforms to the cultural practice of the day.

The ambiguity regarding "form" in Scripture is by unique design. Had the Holy Spirit specified a lot of form when He inspired the New Testament writers to describe New Testament functions, Christians all over the world would be attempting to copy form rather than function. Rather than allowing the biblical objectives to guide us in creating unique forms for a given moment in history and in particular cultures, we would probably be locking ourselves into first-century patterns and structures. This would be lethal to Christianity. The fact is, 20th-century Christians are often guilty of making the Scriptures teach form when it is not even there. Think of what it would be like if there were an abundance of forms spelled out in the New Testament. The Church would really be in trouble.

The Supra-cultural Aspect

It is always appropriate (and important) for Christians to "greet one another." And though we may use the common and accepted form of greeting in a particular culture, it should be a holy form—a form that has deep meaning, reflecting sincere Christian love.

Greetings among people generally tend to be quite empty.

People say, "Hello, how are you?" without any thought of wanting to know how you *really* are. Many people say, "It's been good to see you." Yet they could care less if they ever see you again. Many people say, "I'm glad you came," while not caring if you'll ever come again. All of these, of course, are meaningless and empty, if not in many instances downright dishonest and hypocritical.

Paul's concern (and Peter's) was that these New Testament Christians would greet one another with pure motives. It was to be a true expression of concern and love. And today when Christians greet one another, it must reflect the same dynamic. There is no place for hypocrisy and dishonesty among members of Christ's body.

If we cannot greet one another in this way, we are admonished to confess our sins to each other to "pray for each other," and to forgive one another (James 5:16; Col. 3:13). We are not to be out of harmony with other Christians. If a brother has sinned against us, we are to go to that person and, with grace and love, express our feelings. If we have sinned against someone, we are to ask his forgiveness (Matt. 18:15).

Practical Steps for Helping Christians to Greet One Another in a Biblical Fashion
Step 1
You cannot greet others sincerely if you do not really care about them, or if there is something between you and another Christian brother or sister. The first step in getting back into God's will is to correct that problem. If you have been sinned against, go to that person and share why you feel the way you do. On the other hand, if you have sinned against someone else, immediately take the initiative and ask forgiveness.

Note: Be prepared to discover that you may be as wrong as the other person, though you feel it's all his fault. Bad feelings exist among Christians today because of misunderstandings and a breakdown in communication. Each sincerely feels the other person is wrong. The fact is that both can be wrong!

Step 2
Make a serious effort to develop sincere interest in others. If you don't, you'll never feel comfortable greeting them. You'll always be "running away"—often blaming other people for not being interested in you.

Note: If you have difficulty expressing sincere affection and love for other Christians, your problem may be rooted in one of two sources. Either you are a self-centered person because you always think of yourself first and have built the world around yourself; or perhaps you feel uncomfortable with people because you are fearful. Perhaps you have deep feelings of inferiority.

There is only one basic solution to both of these problems —no matter what the root cause. You must forget about yourself. You must reach out to others. And though it may be painful—especially if your problem is psychological—you must begin to experience the benefits of relational Christianity. If you don't, you will never grow spiritually as you should. Furthermore, you will not be functioning fully as part of the body, helping other people to grow.

Step 3
Consider the aspects of physical affection in greeting other Christians. There is no doubt that first-century Christians greeted one another with more than words. This we can be sure of. A kiss—no matter how performed—involved physical contact with the other person. It probably involved both sexes. Could it be that 20th-century Christians have been so concerned with the "dangers" of touching others of the opposite sex that we have gone to the other extreme?

Note: There *are* dangers when Christians generally show

physical affection to each other, particularly towards the opposite sex. If people are vulnerable to sensuous behavior, they will probably engage in inappropriate thoughts and actions no matter what the situation. There can also be dangers in "just talking" to Christians of the opposite sex.

Following are several guidelines that will help Christians avoid problems in showing physical affection—particularly to those of the opposite sex.

1. Men and women who are not related should *always* be discreet about showing physical affection.

2. Physical affection among unmarried people should rarely be expressed in private situations. People who are seriously looking forward to marriage should guard themselves at all times.

Note: Pastors and professional counselors must be especially cautious about showing physical affection. An emotionally or spiritually sick woman (or man) can destroy another's reputation through gossip. Such a person might exaggerate any show of affection because of vain imagination.

3. Unmarried Christians should never show physical affection in such a way to stimulate the sensuous nature of the other person, causing improper thoughts and actions.

4. Some people who are more vulnerable to sin must always be more cautious than others in showing physical affection to the opposite sex. A young woman once complained to her pastor that her father, who was a Christian involved in Christian work, insisted on sensuously kissing her on the lips. The pastor later discovered that this man had a very unsatisfying relationship with his wife. Obviously, he was vulnerable sexually, even in expressing affection to his own daughter.

A Final Word

Mature Christians can and should show physical affection. In our society, shaking hands, a kiss on the cheek, a gentle embrace are certainly appropriate. Most Christians can express this kind of affection. But this kind of affection must always be based on pure motives, discretion, and above all, true Christian love. When it is expressed in this manner, it can create oneness, unity, and even spiritual and psychological healing. But when it is expressed inappropriately, reflecting impure motives, indiscretion, and selfish actions, it can lead to severe hurt, bitterness, and even immorality. But isn't this true of most every ingredient in Christian relationships?

8

Serve One Another

"You, my brothers, were called to be free. But do not use your freedom to indulge your sinful nature; rather, *serve one another in love*" (Gal. 5:13).

Freedom emerges as a major theme in Paul's letter to the Galatian Christians. No longer are they to "let [themselves] be burdened again by a yoke of slavery" (Gal. 5:1). Formerly, they—along with the whole world—were "prisoners of sin" (3:22). The Law of God thundered from Sinai did not set them free from sin. It simply made them more aware of how captive they were to their old natures. Throughout the years that followed, the law of Moses became God's means "to lead us to Christ that we might be justified by faith" (3:24). It was Christ who fulfilled the requirement of the law—death. Thus Paul could write to the Galatians: "It is for freedom that Christ has set us free" (5:1).

Freedom—What Is It?
What does Paul mean by "freedom in Christ"? First, let's look at what he doesn't mean.

1. Freedom in Christ is not freedom to sin (Gal. 5:13). The Galatians, like so many Christians today, had gone to two extremes. On the one hand, some had reverted to trying to become righteous by keeping the law. This only served to bring them back into bondage (Gal. 5:2-4). On the other hand, some, having heard Paul's teaching about freedom, felt they were now able to do anything they wanted to do. Thus Paul wrote—yes, you are free, *but* "do not use your freedom to indulge your sinful nature" (Gal. 5:13). When dealing with a similar problem, Paul wrote to the Romans: "What shall we say, then? Shall we go on sinning so that grace may increase? *By no means!* We died to sin; how can we live in it any longer?" (Rom. 6:1-2)

Freedom in Christ is not freedom to sin. To have this attitude is to misuse, abuse, and misunderstand the grace of God. Paul, writing to Titus, graphically described what a true view of God's grace will do: "For the grace of God that brings salvation has appeared to all men. It teaches us to say 'No' to *ungodliness* and *worldly passions,* and to live *self-controlled, upright* and *godly lives* in this present age, while we wait for the blessed hope—the glorious appearing of our great God and Saviour, Jesus Christ, who gave Himself for us to redeem us from *all wickedness* and *to purify* for Himself a people that are His very own, eager to do what is good" (Titus 2:11-14).

2. Freedom in Christ is not freedom from the reality of the old nature. Nowhere does the Bible teach that a believer can become perfect—totally free from sin—in this life. When Christ died *for* our sins, He did not, with His death and resurrection, eliminate our sinful natures. Thus Paul had to warn the Galatians *not* to indulge their sinful natures. If these Christians no longer had a sinful nature, Paul wouldn't have needed to warn them against it. There would have been no reason to be so specific about the acts of the old sinful nature.

3. Freedom in Christ is not freedom from servanthood. This is one of Paul's primary points in this Galatian passage. He helps us understand what Christian freedom really is! Rather than using others to indulge our sinful natures, we are to "serve one another in love"—literally, to be slaves or servants to each other.

But, you ask, how can Christians be free and yet be slaves? Herein lies one of the great mysteries of the Christian faith. Jesus spoke about it when He said: "If anyone would come after Me, he must deny himself and take up his cross and follow Me. For whoever wants to *save his life* will lose it, but whoever *loses his life* for Me and for the Gospel will save it" (Mark 8:34-35).

The Christian who wants to experience true *freedom in Christ* must live in total *commitment to Christ*. It sounds paradoxical, but in turning our lives over to Him completely we discover the freedom about which the Bible talks. Paul, of all men, knew freedom in Christ, yet he frequently introduced himself as a servant of Christ (Rom. 1:1; Phil. 1:1; Titus 1:1).

Some Christians stop at this point, not realizing that being a "servant of Christ" also involves them with other members of the body of Christ. Turning our lives over to Christ also means turning our lives over to each other. We are part of a body of which Christ is the head. Being "in Christ" also means being "a part of each other." This is why Paul told the Ephesian Christians to "submit to *one another* out of *reverence* for Christ" (Eph. 5:21; see also 1 Peter 5:5).

Freedom and Human Relationships

Paul's primary concern in this Galatian passage (Gal. 5:13-26) focuses on relational Christianity. Five times he uses the "one another" concept. The first exhortation—the theme of this chapter—is stated positively. We are to "serve one another in love" (5:13). But Paul stated the other four negatively in order to clarify what he really meant. Thus he wrote: "If you keep on biting and devouring *each other*, watch out or you will be destroyed by *each other*" (5:15). Later he said, as he concluded this passage: "Let us not become conceited, provoking [*each other*] and envying *each other*" (5:26).

1. *"The acts of the sinful nature" versus "the fruit of the Spirit"* (Gal. 5:16-18). Human relationships make an interesting study. Sociologists and psychologists spend a lifetime attempting to understand the dynamics involved. And there is much we can learn, even from non-Christians. All truth is God's truth, no matter who discovers it.

Man will never be able to satisfactorily understand and explain the dynamics of human behavior and relationships apart from truth revealed by the Holy Spirit and recorded in the Word of God. Only in the Bible do we discover the reason why people do what they do.

People generally are dominated by a sinful nature. Of course, the way in which that nature expresses itself varies greatly, depending on the influence of Christian truth on particular societies and cultures. Even since Adam and Eve sinned in the Garden of Eden, all men have been afflicted with this spiritual disease (Rom. 5:12-14). All history, both biblical and secular, verifies this doctrine. No matter what man has done to try to improve the world, society eventually deteriorated, primarily because man is sinful and selfish. Rather than desiring to serve others, he desires to serve himself. And even in so-called Christian cultures, social programs —as good as they may be—do not work effectively because mankind is basically selfish and dishonest.

Yet mankind is not doomed to yield to the desires of his sinful nature. Wherever the Christian Gospel penetrates a society, revealing that Christ died for the sins of the world, people discover that they can "live by the Spirit" rather than by the desires of their sinful natures. True, there will be a conflict between the two, even in a Christian's life, but he can now be "led by the Spirit"—rather than by the desires of the flesh. Man can now choose whom he will serve.

2. *Serving one another selfishly* (Gal. 5:19-21). Man was destined to live in relationship to others. Very few people deliberately choose to live an isolated life, because God created man a social creature. The Lord bore witness to this fact from the very beginning when He said: "It is not good for the man to be alone; I will make him a helper suitable for him" (Gen. 2:18, NASB).

When sin entered the human race, man's need for relationships with others did not cease. For several reasons, however, the process was terribly complicated and distorted. First, man became selfish by nature. He came into bondage *to* himself. Second, he was in bondage to the selfishness of others; others were in bondage to his selfishness. He could not live without others, for he was dependent on others to meet his needs. Nor were they able to live without him, for they were dependent on him to meet their needs. Thus we see that there isn't such a thing as *total freedom*. Even non-Christians must "serve one another" in order to survive physically and psychologically. The main problem, of course, is that there was no alternative to selfishness—until Christ provided the way of love.

Interestingly, non-Christians who have been exposed to the effects of the Gospel on culture, can live in relationship to others to a certain extent according to the principles of Scripture. They can even experience some of that "fruit." This we've seen in our nation which was founded upon some of the precepts of Christianity. But as the influence of Christianity is minimized, mankind at large deteriorates rapidly and soon moves in the direction of uncontrolled selfish behavior.

Paul explained to the Galatians, *"the acts of the sinful*

nature are obvious." And note! These acts are in the context of human relationships: "Sexual immorality, impurity and debauchery; idolatry and witchcraft; hatred, discord, jealousy, fits of rage, selfish ambition, dissensions, factions and envy; drunkenness, orgies, and the like" (Gal. 5:19-21).

Till recent years in our own country, these "acts of the sinful nature" were not so glaring. One reason: the influence of biblical truth. But another reason is that man has always had a way of hiding his true nature and what he really does, even in a controlled environment. With the "openness" that has become a way of life in America, we discover even those we least suspect engage in the very "acts of the sinful nature" enumerated by Paul. And most surprising to many Americans—particularly Christians—has been the private (and even public) lives of our presidents and congressmen.

3. *"Serving one another in love."* Though all people must serve one another in order to survive, and though all of us have a sinful nature, there is a way to serve one another that will set us free. This can create very satisfying and lasting relationships. It is the way of love.

By faith in His death and resurrection, we are set free from the domination of our sinful natures. Rather than having to serve one another selfishly, we can actually serve one another *in love*. The acts of this kind of behavior are also obvious. Paul called them the "fruit of the Spirit."

Note again, what Paul enumerates are in the context of relationships. What he describes are not personal emotions but corporate manifestations. When "we serve one another in love" there are, of course, expressions of *love*. There are also expressions of *joy*. There is *peace*—that is, true unity and oneness in the body of Christ. There is *patience* with one another. There is *"kindness, goodness, faithfulness, gentleness, self-control"* (Gal. 5:22-23). These, wrote Paul, are the results of people in relationship who are not serving each other selfishly, but "serving one another in love." When we "live by the Spirit" we "keep in step with the Spirit" (Gal. 5:25). We will no longer "bite and devour one another" and "provoke and envy one another."

In summation, then, we must conclude that freedom in Christ does not give a Christian a right to sin, nor does it eliminate his sinful nature. Neither is man free from responsibility to others. In fact, he has a greater responsibility, because he is now a member of the family of God.

As a member of that family, with all of its rights and privileges, a Christian is to be a servant to all other members of that family. In fact, we are *all* to be servants of one another. And in "serving one another in love" we find true freedom in Jesus Christ. Our deepest needs are met in legitimate ways. We are not used by one another. We are not put on a performance standard. Our relationships with others can be truly satisfying and enduring. This is *true* freedom!

Practical Steps for Helping Other Christians
To Begin Serving One Another in Love
Step 1

Evaluate how much you and others in your church may be reflecting "the acts of the sinful nature" in your relationships rather than "the fruit of the Spirit." One way to get at this information is to begin with the following questions. The answers give indication of Christian maturity in a body of believers. A seven-point scale is included to help you measure various manifestations of Christlikeness. The number "1" signifies that the particular characteristic being evaluated is *never* visible. The number "7" indicates it is *always* visible. The numbers in between represent degrees of visibility.

	Never visible				Always visible		
1. Is there Christian love being expressed among one another in my church?	1	2	3	4	5	6	7
2. Are there evidences of joy and happiness?	1	2	3	4	5	6	7
3. Is there peace, oneness, and unity?	1	2	3	4	5	6	7
4. Are believers showing patience with each other?	1	2	3	4	5	6	7
5. Are they kind in their actions and attitudes?	1	2	3	4	5	6	7
6. Are they demonstrating goodness? (This is done through concrete acts rather than only words.)	1	2	3	4	5	6	7
7. Are they faithful to each other? (This is the opposite of being fickle and untrustworthy.)	1	2	3	4	5	6	7
8. Are they demonstrating gentleness and sensitivity in their relationships with each other?	1	2	3	4	5	6	7

	Never visible				Always visible		
9. Is there self-control in their conversations with each other and in their general life-style?	1	2	3	4	5	6	7

If you have difficulty recognizing these evidences, there can be but one conclusion: more "acts of the sinful nature" are being reflected than the "fruit of the Spirit." When this is true, Christians are not actively "serving one another in love."

Note: Some Christians do not believe the "acts of the old nature" are visible in their church because there is no flagrant sexual immorality, impurity, debauchery, idolatry, witchcraft, drunkenness, and orgies. But they conveniently overlook the fact that the "acts of the old nature" also include hatred, discord, jealousy, fits of rage, selfish ambition, dissention, factions, and envy.

Step 2

In order to check your own objectivity and the accuracy of your observations, ask several Christians in your church to take Step 1. Then prayerfully compare notes.

Step 3

If, as a group, you feel others in your church are not actively "serving one another in love," if the "acts of the sinful nature" are more obvious than "the fruit of the Spirit," then think about taking the following approaches:

First, make sure you are not guilty of allowing your old nature to dominate your own relationships with others.

Second, develop a small group of Christians who will consciously attempt to manifest the fruit of the Spirit.

Third, begin to pray for others in the church—but only after you've made sure your own life is in order.

Fourth, as a larger group, determine to reflect the fruit of the Spirit in all relationships with all other members of the body of Christ.

Warning: Carefully guard against "spiritual pride" and "pseudo-spirituality." Attitudes of superiority and spiritual pride create more problems than solutions.

9

Bear One Another's Burdens

"Bear one another's burdens, and thus fulfil the law of Christ" (Gal. 6:2, NASB).

Dealing with sin in the lives of fellow believers is one of the most difficult tasks God has given Christians. It's much easier to carry out the other injunctions relating to body function. Consequently, many churches ignore this responsibility entirely. Others treat it lightly. Still others deal with the issue of sin only rather than with the individual or individuals involved.

What does the Bible say about the subject? This was Paul's primary concern when he exhorted the Galatians to "carry each other's burdens" (Gal. 6:2). This should not surprise us since he had just discussed in detail what it means to keep in step with the Spirit rather than to engage in the acts of the sinful nature.

Then Paul came right to the point—"Brothers, if a man is trapped in some sin, you who are spiritual should *restore him* gently. But watch yourself; you also may be tempted" (Gal. 6:1).

Paul made the matter crystal clear. Christians *do* have a responsibility when others sin. We have no choice if we wish to be in God's will. We are to attempt to *restore* that person—that is, we are to help that person acknowledge his sin and overcome it.

In this verse Paul gave some specific guidelines for carrying out this process—guidelines that are absolutely essential if there are to be positive results.

Restoration is a Task for Spiritual Christians

Paul wrote: "You who are spiritual shall restore him." Generally speaking, there are two classes of people described in the New Testament—*Christians* and *non-Christians*. But there are also two classes of Christians—*spiritual* and *carnal*. Spiritual Christians "live by the Spirit" and "keep in step with the Spirit," to use Paul's words (Gal. 5:25). They manifest the fruit of the Spirit in their relationships with one another: love, joy, peace, patience, kindness, goodness, faithfulness, gentleness, and self-control (Gal. 5:22-23).

Carnal Christians are Christians, but sometimes it's difficult to tell. In many respects, they live like non-Christians—according to "the acts of the sinful nature." The Corinthians exemplified this category. Paul knew they were true believers because he had seen evidences of God's grace in their lives. When they were converted, they were, as no other New Testament church, endowed with spiritual gifts. Thus Paul began his letter, "I always thank God for you because of His grace given you in Christ Jesus. For in Him you have been enriched in every way—in all your *speaking* and in all your knowledge—because our testimony about Christ was confirmed in you. Therefore, you do not lack any *spiritual gift*" (1 Cor. 1:4-7).

But Paul hastened to say that when he was among them he could not talk to them as spiritual, but he had to speak to them as carnal Christians. Many months later, as he penned his first letter to the Corinthians, he still could not address them as spiritual. They were still carnal: "Brothers, I could not address you as spiritual but as worldly [carnal]—mere infants in Christ. I gave you milk, not solid food, for you were not ready for it. Indeed, you are still not ready. You are still worldly [carnal]. For since there is jealousy and quarreling among you, are you not worldly? Are you not acting like mere men? [that is, as non-Christians]" (1 Cor. 3:1-3).

Paul's description of the Corinthians' behavior with one another—their jealousy and quarreling—correlates, of course, with what he described in his Galatian letter as the "acts of the sinful nature." They were still "walking in the flesh" rather than "in the Spirit." Their relationships with each other were anything but reflections of the Holy Spirit's guidance and fruit.

But back to Paul's Galatian letter. Here the apostle emphasized that dealing with sin in the life of a carnal Christian certainly was not a task for others who were also carnal. Rather, he wrote, "You who are *spiritual* shall restore him" (6:1). True, *all* Christians are responsible to minister to each other, but only those in the body of Christ who are walking in God's will are to deal with sin in the lives of others. This is why Jesus spoke so pointedly about this matter: "Can a blind man lead a blind man? Will they not both fall into a pit? . . . Why do you look at the speck of sawdust in your brother's eye and pay no attention to the plank in your own eye? How can you say to your brother, 'Brother, let me take the speck out of your eye,' when you yourself fail to see the plank in your own eye? You hypocrite, first take the plank out of your eye, and then you will see clearly to remove the speck from your brother's eye" (Luke 6:39, 41-42).

This, of course, puts a very heavy responsibility on pastors and elders in the church. If you are a leader in your church you must constantly make sure you are reflecting Jesus Christ in your own life. This is why James warned: "Not many of you should act as teachers, my brothers, because you know that we who teach will be judged more strictly" (James 3:1).

But note when Paul wrote to the Galatians that restoring a person who is "trapped in some sin" was a task for *spiritual Christians,* he did not mean it was a job only for the leaders of the church. Rather, it is a responsibility for *all* Christians. Furthermore, this is not an excuse for Christians to remain carnal. To be in the will of God, we must grow and become like Jesus Christ. The Apostle Peter made this clear when he wrote: "Therefore, rid yourselves of all malice and all deceit, hypocrisy, jealousy, and slander of every kind. Like newborn babies, crave pure spiritual milk, so that by it you may grow up in your salvation" (1 Peter 2:1-2).

In summary, then, spiritual Christians have a definite responsibility to help carnal Christians—especially those who are "trapped in some sin." But even further, we have a responsibility not to *cause* them to sin. Paul wrote to the Romans: "We who are strong ought to bear with the failings of the weak, and not to please ourselves. Each of us should please his neighbor for his good, to build him up" (Rom. 15:1-2; see also 1 Cor. 8:9).

Restoration Is a Task for More Than One Person

Paul directed this exhortation at more than one member of the church. He used a plural pronoun when he wrote "*you* who *are* spiritual shall restore him." Jesus Christ outlined a very important procedure when dealing with sin in the life of another Christian. He said: "If your brother sins against you, go and show him his fault, just between the two of you. If he listens to you, you have won your brother over. But if he will not listen, take one or two others along, so that 'every matter may be established by the testimony of two or three witnesses.' If he refuses to listen to them, tell it to the church; and if he refuses to listen even to the church, treat him as you would a pagan or a tax collector" (Matt. 18:15-17).

In this passage Jesus specifically outlined the procedure for handling sin in the life of someone who has sinned against another Christian on a personal basis. In such cases, correction is to be on a one-on-one basis also. You are not to talk to others, but directly to the person who has sinned against you. However, if he will not listen, then take several others with you when you talk with him again.

Carl had spread rumors that Dale was going bankrupt. Because clients were cautious about giving long-term contracts to Dale, they switched to Carl's firm. Carl laughed when Dale confronted him about the spreading of such falsehoods. But when Dale took two of the church elders and his accountant to see Carl, Carl soon realized his error and asked for forgiveness. He also promised to stop soliciting any business from Dale's clients and to inform them of Dale's solvency.

There are also sins that cannot be categorized as sins against another Christian. Rather, they are sins against the whole Christian family. In these cases, Paul indicates that a carnal Christian should be approached by several spiritual Christians immediately. Thus he wrote: "*You* [plural] who are spiritual should restore him."

This, of course, has some very practical ramifications. This kind of task calls for corporate wisdom and strength. In some instances, as we'll see, it is dangerous to tackle the problem alone.

Restoration Is a Task to be Done with Genuine Humility
"Restore him gently!" wrote Paul. In essence, he was referring to *humility*. Thus he wrote later: "If anyone thinks he is something when he is nothing, he deceives himself" (Gal. 6:1, 3).

Christians who approach another Christian about sin must do so with a great sense of their own unworthiness to be called children of God. In fact, Paul made it clear to Titus that we are to even approach non-Christians in this way—"to show true humility toward *all* men." Then he explained why. "At one time we too were foolish, disobedient, deceived and enslaved by all kinds of passions and pleasures. We lived in malice and envy, being hated and hating one another. But when the kindness and love of God our Saviour appeared, He saved us, not because of righteous things we had done, but because of His mercy" (Titus 3:2-5).

In other words, Paul was exhorting Titus to remind the Christians at Crete to approach everyone with a true sense of understanding and humility. Christians should always remember that it was only God's grace that had saved them when they were yet in their sins. Putting it even more specifically: no saved person who truly understands the grace of God in his own life can approach any person with arrogance, pride, or a sense of superiority.

Paul's concern in writing this portion to the Galatians was how to help Christians who were "trapped in some sin." He admonished all spiritual Christians to approach that person with an attitude of true gentleness and humility. In so doing they would help carry that person's burden with the same attitude Christ approached us while we were yet in our sins. This is why Paul himself appealed to the Corinthians—who were trapped in *many* sins—"by the meekness and gentleness of Christ" (2 Cor. 10:1).

The Apostle included his most extensive elaboration regarding this concept in his second letter to Timothy. He warned this young man to avoid getting into quarrels with people who were opposing the truth of God. Rather, he wrote, "be *kind* to everyone, able to teach, not resentful. Those who oppose him he must gently instruct [with patience and humility], in the hope that God will give them a change of heart leading them to a knowledge of the truth, and that they will come to their senses and escape from the *trap* of the devil, who has taken them captive to do his will" (2 Tim. 2:24-26).

There is no more effective approach than a gentle, compassionate, kind and patient approach when dealing with another person (Col. 3:12). A harsh, bitter, insensitive approach only threatens the person who is at fault. Since Christians in this condition are already weak and very guilty, they will usually not respond positively to a strong, negative encounter. Such an approach may only make the problem worse.

We've all made mistakes in dealing with sin in the lives of other Christians—as a parent with his children, as a pastor with his people, or as one Christian with another. I've had the best response confronting those who are out of fellowship with God when I acted in harmony with Paul's injunctions to treat others with gentleness, humility, and meekness. I've had negative responses when I was insensitive, too quick to judge, and too harsh in my words. I may have been right in my observations, but wrong in the *way* I went about seeking to correct the person who had sinned.

But note that some carnal Christians will not respond to this approach—no matter how humble, kind, and gentle you are. Fortunately, most will, but there are exceptions. Paul was on the verge of having to face the exceptions when he first wrote to the Corinthians and dealt with their sins. So, he gave them a choice. "What do you prefer?" he asked. "Shall I come to you with punishment, or in love and with a gentle spirit?" (1 Cor. 4:21) Some Christians are so caught up in their sins, so self-deceived, and so arrogant that they will not respond to a gentle approach. If they do not, we must then take a second step in church discipline—to break fellowship with that kind of Christian.

Here Paul pulled no punches with the Corinthians: "But now I am writing to you that you must not associate with anyone who calls himself a brother but is sexually immoral or greedy, an idolator or a slanderer, a drunkard or a swindler. With such a man do not even eat" (1 Cor. 5:11).

This was the final step, and Paul's firmness in love brought unusual results. The Corinthians dealt with the man in their midst who was living in flagrant immorality. Evidently they also came to grips with their own sin. Thus Paul could write in his second letter: "Godly sorrow brings repentance. . . . See what this godly sorrow has produced in you" (2 Cor. 7:10-11). And then, too, the immoral man who was expelled from their midst also became repentant. In a Christlike fashion, Paul exhorted them to forgive the man, to receive him back, love him, and encourage him in the Christian faith (2 Cor. 2:5-8).

In summary, then, spiritual Christians are responsible to help carnal Christians overcome their problems with sin. But we are to restore them gently—with humility and meekness.

Restoration Must Be Done Cautiously

When several Christians, even spiritual Christians, approach someone to help him escape from the trap of sin, it must be done carefully. "Watch yourself," warned Paul. "You also may be tempted" (Gal. 6:1).

The lusts of the flesh are very deceptive—and very attractive. And some Christians, when attempting to help another believer who is trapped in some sin, soon find themselves participating in the same sins. This Paul warned against.

Some pastors and Christian counselors have attempted to help women who are having sexually oriented problems and end up as a part of the moral problem. They allowed themselves to be open to temptation—or took advantage of the one who came for counsel. How tragic! And what a warning to every Christian!

Not long ago, a well-known Christian leader—an outstanding evangelist and president of a well-known Christian college, became involved with one of the women students. Eventually he divorced his wife and left the ministry altogether to live with this young woman. What a pity! And how devastating to the Christian community.

How easy it is for a well-meaning Christian, particularly one who is weak in certain areas of life, to fall into Satan's trap. This is particularly tragic when the person is attempting to help another Christian overcome his sin. We have a responsibility to carry each others' burdens, but we must do so very carefully. We must make sure we are mature enough to be able to handle the problem. This, of course, is the primary reason why Paul wrote, *"You who are spiritual* should restore him gently."* And even then we must watch ourselves, since we may also be tempted.

Yet we must not let a fear of personal failure keep us from fulfilling God's will towards other Christians. Most of us, even if we are spiritual, know our areas of vulnerability. In some instances it would be wise to have another Christian who is stronger than we are in certain areas help us handle certain problems in the lives of others. Then, too, there are problems where we should *always* have more than one person involved in the confrontation—particularly when dealing with a sexual problem. We must remember, for example, that a person who is immoral sexually may also be a persistent liar. Some carnal Christians have falsely accused other Christians who have tried to help them, thus marring the helper's reputation also.

Yes, we must be on guard for temptation in our own lives when we attempt to help a carnal Christian. But thank God for Paul's promise to the Corinthians—and to us: "No temptation has seized you except what is common to man. And God is faithful; He will not let you be tempted beyond what you can bear. But when you are tempted, He will also provide a way out so that you can stand up under it" (1 Cor. 10:13).

Restoration Must Be Done Prayerfully

James adds an important dimension to the process involved in bearing the sin burdens of other Christians. "Confess your sins to each other," he wrote in his epistle. Then he spelled out why: "And pray for each other so that you may be healed" (James 5:16).

When a Christian indulges in sin, when he "sows to please his sinful nature," he will from that nature, "reap destruction" (Gal. 6:7-8). Obviously a non-Christian who does not turn to Christ but continues in his sin will end up spending eternity without Christ. But "destruction" also involves Christians who do not keep in step with the Spirit, but rather, indulge in the acts of the sinful nature. There is inevitable deterioration in their lives—spiritually, psychologically, and physically.

James seems to indicate that some Christians were physically ill because of sin. (Note that James does not say that all illness is caused by specific sin. Rather, he wrote, "*If* he has sinned, he will be forgiven" [5:15].) This, of course, correlates with Paul's observations regarding some of the Corinthian Christians who were living carnal lives. In this case, they were partaking of the Lord's Supper in an unworthy manner. "That is why," wrote Paul, "many among you are weak and sick, and a number of you have fallen asleep"— that is, *died!* (1 Cor. 11:30).

James encouraged believers who were living in sin, and who were sick because of that sin, to confess to other Christians so they could pray with them. Generally, though not exclusively, this was to involve the elders of the church. Earlier in the paragraph, James wrote: "Is any one of you sick? He should call the elders of the church to pray over him and anoint him with oil in the name of the Lord. And the prayer offered in faith will make the sick person well; the Lord will raise him up. If he has sinned, he will be forgiven" (James 5:14-15).

Restoring a Christian, then, should involve prayer. And prayers can be quite particular if the effects of sin have become obvious in the individual's personality. There is no reason why Christians in the 20th century should not follow the practice of having the elders of the church anoint with oil and pray for the sick—no matter what the cause of the illness. God, of course, does not promise to heal all believers, but He does honor obedience and faith. And in many instances, if it is according to His will, He will actually heal. Sometimes in dramatic ways!

Practical Steps for Dealing with Sin in the Lives of Other Christians
Step 1
Evaluate your own life. Are you among those who are spiritual? That is, are you ordering your life by the Spirit, keeping in step with the Spirit? Are you living in such a way, and in relationship to other Christians, that the fruit of the Spirit is obvious in your life?

Check yourself! If you classify yourself among those who are spiritual, you will reflect love and joy; you will be at peace with other Christians; you will demonstrate patience, kindness, goodness, faithfulness, gentleness, and self-control (Gal. 5:22-23).

And whatever you do, remember Jesus' words, "Don't try to take the speck of sawdust out of your brother's eye when you have a two-by-four in your own" (see Matt. 7:4).

Step 2
Make sure you are evaluating another Christian's life-style

from a true biblical perspective. Some Christians go around compulsively looking for sin in other Christians' lives. Some Christians are expert at making up "extra-biblical" lists to help them evaluate sins. This, of course, can quickly lead to judging others (see Rom. 14:13). Of course, judging is sin in itself. It reflects a pharisaical attitude.

On the other hand, Christians are to be concerned for those Christians who become trapped in some sin. In love they are to gently, cautiously, and prayerfully restore such persons.

Not surprisingly, just before Paul admonished Christians to "bear one another's burdens," he catalogued the "acts of the sinful nature" (Gal. 5:19-21). This list in turn became a biblical criterion for determining what is indeed sin in a believer's life. This is a supra-cultural list, guideline for all time.

Note: On page 90 are four lists, representing four translations. This is done to enable you to discover more specific definitions of what Paul listed. Some of the Greek words he used tend to be general and interrelated. The four viewpoints will help you determine more accurately what Paul was saying.

Step 3

Once you have evaluated your own life-style and have made sure you have biblical grounds for evaluating another Christian's actions as sins, you are then ready to follow biblical procedures in confronting that Christian about his sin.

There are three levels of disciplinary action in the New Testament. First, we are to warn a Christian about his sin, attempting to restore him and release him from Satan's trap (1 Thes. 5:14; Gal. 6:1-2). If a person does not respond and turn from his sin, then we are not to fellowship with that Christian (2 Thes. 3:6, 14). The final step is excommunication—to actually consider this person as if he were an unbeliever (Matt. 18:17).

It has been my experience that when one follows proper

KJV	NIV	NASB	Beck
adultery & fornication	sexual immorality	immorality	sexual sin
uncleanness	impurity	impurity	uncleanness
lasciviousness	debauchery	sensuality	wild living
idolatry	idolatry	idolatry	worshiping of idols
witchcraft	witchcraft	sorcery	witchcraft
hatred	hatred	enmities	hate
variance	discord	strife	wrangling
emulations	jealousy	jealousy	jealousy
wrath	fits of rage	outbursts of anger	anger
strife	selfish ambition	disputes	selfishness
seditions	dissensions	dissensions	quarreling
heresies	factions	factions	divisions
envyings, murders	envy	envyings	envy
drunkenness	drunkenness	drunkenness	drunkenness
revellings	orgies	carousings	carousing

procedure in dealing with sin in the lives of other Christians, it is seldom necessary to go beyond the first level. Unfortunately, it is at this initial level that we frequently fail to act. Furthermore, it is this *first* level that Paul had in mind when he said we are to "bear one another's burdens." And for what purpose? In order to restore the person who is trapped in sin. This is the true purpose of all discipline, no matter on what level we're operating. Discipline must always be done in love and with the purpose of helping the person turn from his sin and to once again "keep in step with the Spirit" rather than engage in "the acts of the sinful nature."

10

Bearing with One Another

"Be completely humble and gentle; be patient, *bearing with one another* in love" (Eph. 4:2).

In the previous chapter, we studied Paul's injunction to the Galatians to "bear one another's burdens." In his Ephesian letter we discover another injunction that sounds very similar but in meaning is quite different. We are to "bear with one another in love." In Galatians, Paul was talking about helping another Christian to bear *(bastazō)* or carry his burden of sin; to help him get out of Satan's trap. But in Ephesians, the word *bear* means to be tolerant towards other Christians; to *bear* with them; to patiently endure their idiosyncrasies and weaknesses; to have a forgiving spirit toward others who may sin against us.

I'm fortunate, I guess. I enjoy people. Since I have a pretty good picture of my own weaknesses, I find it rather easy to tolerate most people. Yet as I reflect on my past and present relationships with Christians, a few faces come to mind who represent what some might term as "unlovable." To be perfectly honest, I must admit it was at times difficult to bear with them.

For example, I remember John, probably one of the most difficult. He was a college roommate whose middle name was Mr. Self-Centered. This was not simply my opinion; most people who knew him well agreed! He was just plain hard to get along with.

But he was a Christian—a brother in Christ. And I had a responsibility to John—"to bear with him in love" (Eph. 4:2). Paul's letter to the Colossians made my responsibility even clearer: "Therefore, as God's chosen people, holy and dearly loved, clothe yourselves with compassion, kindness, humility, gentleness and patience. *Bear with each other* and forgive whatever grievances you may have against one another. Forgive as the Lord forgave you" (Col. 3:12-13).

How could I help John? What did Paul really mean when he exhorted Christians to "bear with one another in love"?

Patience

In both passages where Paul exhorted Christians to "bear with one another," the key word preceding this injunction is *patience.* The King James Version uses the word "longsuffering," one aspect of "walking in the Spirit" (Gal. 5:22). It is also the focus of Paul's prayer for the Colossian Christians: "And we pray this . . . so that you may have *great endurance* and *patience,* and joyfully giving thanks to the Father, who has qualified you to share in the inheritance of the saints in the kingdom of light" (Col. 1:10-12).

To "bear with one another," then, means being patient with each other's weaknesses. Not one of us is perfect. All of us fail, particularly in human relationships. How easy it is to expect more from other Christians than we expect from ourselves.

This has particular relevance to Christian family living. In the family setting we get to know others like in no other social unit. We live together day after day, week after week, year after year. As members of a family unit we are seen at our best and at our worst—both as parents and as children. Parents often expect more from their children than they do from themselves. Children often expect more from their parents than from other adults in their lives. And together, this dynamic often erupts in anything but patience and forbearance with one another.

The same is often true in the family of God. In a church where people get to know each other as they should, they also get to know each other's idiosyncrasies. This is the challenge Paul gives to us: We are to "bear with one another in love."

When we are tempted to be impatient with one another, we need to think about Jesus Christ and His attitude towards us. This was Paul's secret. The Lord's longsuffering and patience toward him marked his life (1 Tim. 1:15-17) and gave him unusual tolerance toward others. Seeing himself as the worst of sinners and experiencing God's love and patience in saving him caused Paul to respond to others with the love and patience of Jesus Christ.

A Forgiving Spirit

Bearing with one another and having a forgiving spirit are synonymous concepts. This Paul made clear in his Colossian letter. "Bear with each other," he said, "and *forgive* whatever grievances you may have against one another. *Forgive* as the Lord *forgave* you" (Col. 3:13).

Some Christians carry grudges for years. How miserable! And how tragic! And how out of character for a follower of Jesus Christ. How ungrateful for a Christian to hold a grudge against a fellow believer when Christ has canceled our own debt of sin.

Pastor Jones visited in the homes of Christians who had stopped attending his church. Several years before he came as pastor, these people had been offended, sometimes by seemingly insignificant things such as their child's name being left out of a printed Christmas program. They quit coming . . . and continue to live miserable lives by holding grudges against some other member of the church.

One day Peter came to Jesus and asked, " 'Lord, how many times should I forgive my brother when he sins against me? Up to seven times?'

"Jesus answered, 'I tell you, not seven times, but seventy-seven times' " (Matt. 18:21-22).

Jesus then told a story to get His point across:

Therefore, the kingdom of heaven is like a king who wanted to settle accounts with his servants. As he began the settlement, a man who owed him ten thousand talents was brought to him. Since he was not able to pay, the master ordered that he and his wife and his children and all that he had be sold to repay the debt.

The servant fell on his knees before him. "Be patient with me," he begged, "and I will pay back everything." The servant's master took pity on him, canceled the debt and let him go.

But when that servant went out, he found one of his fellow servants who owed him a hundred denarii. He grabbed him and began to choke him. "Pay back what you owe me!" he demanded.

His fellow servant fell to his knees and begged him, "Be patient with me, and I will pay you back."

But he refused. Instead, he went off and had the man thrown into prison until he could pay the debt. When the other servants saw what had happened, they were greatly distressed and went and told their master everything that had happened.

Then the master called the servant in. "You wicked servant," he said, "I canceled all that debt of yours because you begged me to. Shouldn't you have had mercy on your fellow servant just as I had on you?" In anger his master turned him over to the jailers until he paid back all he owed.

This is how my heavenly Father will treat each of you unless you forgive your brother from your heart (Matt. 18:23-35).

Work Hard at Bearing with One Another

Immediately following Paul's injunction to "be patient, bearing with one another in love," he said, *"Make every effort* to keep the unity of the Spirit through the bond of peace" (Eph. 4:2-3).

Patience, forbearance, and forgiveness are not automatic actions that follow conversion to Christ. These involve deliberate acts of the will.

Every person I know who has an unforgiving spirit chooses to do so. And often he chooses to let the other person know how he feels—by avoiding that person, by using cutting and sharp words, by talking behind the person's back. This is *deliberate* action.

Christians who really care about each other, who really are concerned about doing the will of God at all times, will "make every effort to keep the unity of the Spirit through the bond of peace." This is Christianity in action.

Practical Steps for Bearing with One Another in Love
Step 1

Take a good look at yourself. In all honesty, make a list of your weaknesses and idiosyncrasies. These questions will help you.

1. What do I do (or not do) at home that irritates my wife and children (or if single, my parents, my brothers, and my sisters, or apartment-mate)?
2. What do I do (or not do) at work and/or school that

irritates fellow employees and/or teachers and fellow students?

3. What do I do (or not do) that irritates my friends?

Step 2

Now that you have isolated some of your own weaknesses, evaluate these weaknesses in the light of your attitudes and actions towards other Christians. Do you expect more from them than you do from yourself? Do you criticize others in the areas of your own weaknesses?

Note: If you are normal, you probably will have to answer "yes" to both of these questions. Honestly looking at ourselves helps to make us tolerant of others' weaknesses.

Step 3

Make a list of all Christians you have difficulty relating to —especially those you hold a grudge against.

If you can't think of any, praise the Lord! Don't drudge up any just to be practical. But make sure you're being honest.

Now that you've made a list, ask yourself *why* you can't relate to these Christians; or why you are angry at them. Is it because of something they've done to hurt you? Are they aware of how you feel? Are your feelings justified? Or is it because of your imagination and an over-sensitive response on your part? Or are you upset with them because they remind you so much of yourself?

Some Christians are super-sensitive and feel deep hurt at what they interpret to be the slightest rejection. And sometimes, people don't even realize they've hurt someone. For example, I was told one time that someone was hurt because I walked by them without saying "hello." They thought I had snubbed them. Frankly, I had not even remembered the incident. One thing I did know, however, and that was that I had not deliberately snubbed them. Actually, I probably had something else on my mind and completely overlooked their presence.

But I talked to that person just the same. I also sincerely apologized for my absentmindedness. Needless to say, the results were positive—and I also was able to minister to one who had been hurt and over-sensitive.

Step 4

This step is the most difficult to take. But you must do it. Consciously and deliberately forgive every person who has ever done anything to hurt you. Then, one by one, talk to these Christians about whom you feel badly. If they hurt *you* tell them *why* you feel as you do. Ask them to forgive you for your attitude—even though they may be primarily at fault.

Warning: Don't base your "forgiveness" on the condition that they offer an apology. Take care of your own attitudes and God will take care of theirs.

Note: If a Christian has sinned against you (and others) in such a way that it demands a repentant response, and if you have approached that person in love *without* a response, then you'll need to follow the procedure Jesus outlined in Matthew 18:15-17. Make sure, however, that your approach is characterized by "compassion, kindness, humility, gentleness, and patience" (Col. 3:12). If it is, chances are you'll get a positive response.

Remember John? One day I had to approach him about his self-centeredness, his insensitive actions, and his overbearing attitude. The results, eventually, were dramatic. He responded. And so did I. We both learned something about each other's weaknesses—and about our own!

Remember, too, that a Christian is never justified to take the law into his own hands. Listen to Paul: "Do not repay anyone evil for evil. Be careful to do what is right in the sight of everybody. If it is possible, as far as it depends on you, live at peace with everyone. Do not take revenge, my friends, but leave room for God's wrath, for it is written, 'It is Mine to avenge, I will repay,' says the Lord. On the contrary: 'If your enemy is hungry, feed him; if he is thirsty, give him something to drink. In doing this, you will heap burning coals on his head.' Do not be overcome by evil, but overcome evil with good" (Rom. 12:17-21).

11

Submit to One Another

"Submit to one another out of reverence for Christ"
(Eph. 5:21).

Ask the average Christian what he thinks of when he hears
the word "submission" and generally the response will have
something to do with marriage—particularly the attitude and
actions that a wife should have toward her husband. One reason for this, of course, is that the Bible does refer to wifely
submission. On three occasions, Paul exhorts wives to "submit to your husbands" (Eph. 5:22; Col. 3:18; Titus 2:5).
Peter does the same in his first epistle (1 Peter 3:1).

Another reason the average Christian thinks in terms of the
marriage relationship when he hears the word "submission" is
that we have overlooked its larger use in the New Testament.
It is not a word used exclusively to describe a wife's behavior
toward her husband.

Submission—What Does It Mean?
"Submission" is in essence a synonym for "obedience." In its
most general use, it means to yield to another's admonition
and advice. In Scripture it appears in contexts describing ser-

vanthood, humility, respect, reverence, honor, teachableness, and openness. All these for one basic purpose—obedience to Jesus Christ.

This word is also used in relationships of one Christian with another. We are to "submit to *one another*."

The concept of "submission" is used by biblical writers to describe a *variety* of Christian relationships. Paul exhorted *all* Christians (both men and women) to "submit to one another" (Eph. 5:21). This is amplified further when Peter exhorted young men to "be submissive to those who are older" (1 Peter 5:5). All members of Christ's body are exhorted to "obey your leaders and submit to their authority" (Heb. 13:17). Servants are instructed to submit to their masters (Titus 2:9; Eph. 6:5; Col. 3:22; 1 Peter 2:18). This submissiveness applies when serving under either Christian or non-Christian masters. Children, of course, are admonished to obey and submit to their parents (Eph. 6:1; Col. 3:20). And what may surprise those who know little about the Bible is that Christians are also instructed to submit to other authority figures in their lives who are not Christians—particularly those who are leaders in government (Rom. 13:1; 1 Peter 2:13).

We must hasten to add that Christians who are in positions of authority must also function with a submissive attitude. Husbands are directed to love their wives "just as Christ loved the church" (Eph. 5:25). Fathers are to deal sensitively with their children, understanding and meeting their needs (Eph. 6:4; Col. 3:21). Elders are commissioned to be "servants." And they are to "be eager to serve" (1 Peter 5:2). They are not to lord it over other Christians, using their positions as a means of unjust gain—either financially, psychologically, or socially (1 Peter 5:1-4). Christian masters are to treat their servants fairly and sensitively just as Christ treated us when He gave Himself for us (Eph. 6:9; Col. 4:1). In other words,

Paul and Peter are simply reiterating what Jesus Christ taught and demonstrated with His own life.

When Jesus Christ was on earth, He said to His disciples one day when they were arguing among themselves regarding who was to be the greatest in His kingdom: "You know that the *rulers* of the Gentiles lord it over them, and their *high officials* exercise authority over them. Not so with you. Instead, whoever wants to become great among you must be *your servant*, and whoever wants to be first must be *your slave*—just as the Son of Man did not come to be served, but to serve, and to give His life a ransom for many" (Matt. 20:25-28).

Mutual submission, even by those who are in authority, is a distinctive concept made possible by Jesus Christ. Christianity, then, is unique. When Christ came into this world, He brought into being a whole new approach to functional relationships between people. In the "Gentile world," as Jesus called it, there is no such thing as mutual submission. Man basically operates out of selfish motives. He has little or no interest in helping others reach their goals—except when it might benefit himself. He may listen to someone else's advice, but usually not out of respect and honor. Rather, he has discovered that this is the way to develop his own potential and to achieve personal success. Obedience and submission become a means to a selfish end.

In Christ all believers have the potential to "submit to one another out of reverence for Christ." Even those who have positions of authority—elders, husbands, masters [and in our day employers]—are to relate to others with an attitude of submission.

This is what Christ demonstrated for us, when He, the Lord of the universe, became a servant to all men. He, "Who, being in very nature God, did not consider equality with God something to be grasped, but made Himself nothing" (Phil.

2:6-7). Paul made it clear that all Christians—even those in authority—are to follow Christ's example. We are to love as Christ loved. We are to "do nothing out of selfish ambition or vain conceit, but in humility consider others better than ourselves." We are to "look not only to our own interests, but also to the interests of others" (Phil. 2:3-4). We are to "submit to one another *out of reverence for Christ*"—the One who set the perfect example. Our attitude "should be the same as that of Christ Jesus" (Phil. 2:5).

Unfortunately, not all Christians in positions of authority have the mind of Christ. Some men use the concepts of submission and headship to lord it over their wives and others, to *force* them into subservient roles. In reality, they have used the Bible as a means to get their own way. This is not "loving as Christ loved." It's selfishness. Such men have yet to learn that you cannot *demand* respect. For it to be real and meaningful, it must be earned.

Some pastors and other Christian leaders behave toward other members of the body of Christ in the way some men behave toward their wives. They've allowed their position of authority, their educational advantage, and their biblical role to become a means for "putting down" other people and for keeping them in a position of servitude. This is in direct violation of Scripture. To be an "elder worthy of double honor" (1 Tim. 5:17) should mean that we who are in the ministry are greater servants. This indeed is what Christ exemplified in His ministry on earth.

Mutual Submission—Some Biblical Guidelines

Paul made it very clear that submission to other Christians should not be based on subjective impulses and reactions. Rather, the guidelines for mutual submission are rooted in the authority of Jesus Christ and His Word. Thus in a parallel passage Paul exhorted the Colossians: "Let the *Word of*

Christ dwell in you richly as you teach and counsel one another with all wisdom, and as you sing psalms, hymns and
spiritual songs with gratitude in your hearts to God. And
whatever you do, whether in word or deed, do it all *in the
name of the Lord Jesus"* (Col. 3:16-17).

No Christian has the right to request something of another
Christian that is not based in the Word of God. To do so is to
be guilty of judging. And this we must not do (Rom. 14:13).
Christians who exhort others in an erroneous manner are
themselves out of the will of God. This is why Paul, before
issuing a directive to "submit to one another," unequivocally
admonished *all* the Ephesian Christians to be careful how
they lived: "not as unwise but as wise . . . Do not be foolish," he wrote, "but understand what the Lord's will is. Do
not get drunk on wine. . . . Instead, be filled with the Spirit."
Paul implied that only then can Christians properly "speak to
one another with psalms, hymns and spiritual songs." Only
then can they experience the benefits of mutual submission
(Eph. 5:15-21).

Practical Steps for Implementing This Directive in Your Church
The following project is designed to help Christians in your
church submit to one another.

Step 1
Mutual submission must begin with the leadership of the
church. What Paul was teaching must be modeled before all
other members of the local body. If there is contention and
lack of harmony in the pastoral staff and among elders and
deacons, it will become obvious to all other members of the
local Christian family. Just as tension between a husband and
wife cannot be hidden from children, so lack of oneness
among leaders of a church cannot be hidden from the rest of
the congregation.

The converse is also true. A group of leaders who are truly one in Christ become a dynamic example for those for whom they are responsible. The love and unity they experience and demonstrate at the leadership level will filter through the whole church.

The following questions will assist each of your church leaders (and every member of the body) to evaluate his or her attitudes and actions:

1. How do I view others in the church who are in positions of leadership? Do I respect them and honor them as fellow members of Christ's body? Or do I feel I am more important than they are?
2. How do I react when someone disagrees with me? Am I threatened? Do I respond emotionally and defensively? Do I insist on doing things my own way?
3. How often have I admitted to others I have been wrong? Do I always have to be right to feel comfortable?
4. Do I ever share my inner life and struggles with other church leaders? Do I keep my weaknesses to myself?

Note: The key to unity and mutual submission among leaders in the church is to select these leaders on the basis of the spiritual qualifications outlined in 1 Timothy 3:1-7 and Titus 1:5-10. It has been my experience as a pastor that the more seriously we take these qualifications, the more mutual respect, love, and concern there is among believers.

Step 2

All believers must clearly understand the teaching of Scripture regarding the subject of submission. It is not only a directive for wives, but for all members of Christ's body. We must realize that it is possible for husbands to submit to their wives without giving up their headship; for elders to submit to others in Christ's body without giving up their position of authority; that parents can listen to their children's viewpoints without giving up parental status; for employers to give employees careful consideration without losing respect.

The key is for all Christians to develop the mind of Christ, to be willing to lose their lives in order to find them again.

Step 3

Following are the Scriptures that teach submission and obedience to others. Note the variety of relationships in the context of each directive. The words and phrases that are italicized will help you understand what is involved in being a submissive Christian. Use these Scriptures as criteria for evaluating your own attitude toward other members of Christ's body. *Circle* the areas that apply to you and where you feel you are strong. *Underscore* the areas where you feel you are weak.

Elders to Other Members of Christ's Body

"Be shepherds of God's flock that is under your care, *serving* as overseers—not because you *must*, but because you are *willing,* as God wants you to be; not *greedy* for money, but *eager to serve*; not *lording* it over those entrusted to you, but being *examples* to the flock" (1 Peter 5:2-3).

Christians in General to Elders

"The elders who direct the affairs of the church well are worthy of *double honor,* especially those whose work is preaching and teaching. For the Scripture says, "Do not muzzle the ox while it is treading out the grain,' and 'The worker deserves his wages.' *Do not entertain an accusation against an elder unless it is brought by two or three witnesses. Those who sin are to be rebuked publicly, so that the others may take warning*" (1 Timothy 5:17-20).

"*Obey* your leaders and *submit* to their authority. They keep watch over you as men who must give an account. *Obey them* so that their work will be a joy, not a burden, for that would be of no advantage to you" (Heb. 13:17).

Younger Men to Older Men

"Young men, in the same way be *submissive* to those who are older. Clothe yourselves with *humility* toward one another, because, 'God opposes the *proud* but gives grace to the *humble.*' Humble yourselves, therefore, under God's mighty hand, that He may lift you up in due time" (1 Peter 5:5-6).

Husbands to Wives

"Husbands, *love* your wives, just as Christ *loved* the church and *gave Himself* up for her. . . . Husbands ought to love their wives as their own bodies. He who loves his wife loves himself" (Eph. 5:25, 28).

"Husbands, *love* your wives and *do not be harsh with them*" (Col. 3:19).

"Husbands, in the same way *be considerate* as you live with your wives and treat them *with respect* as the weaker partner and as *heirs with you* of the gracious gift of life, so that nothing will hinder your prayers" (1 Peter 3:7).

"The husband should fulfill *his marital duty* to his wife, and likewise the wife to her husband. A wife's body does not belong to her alone but also to her husband. In the same way, a husband's body does not belong to him alone but also to his wife" (1 Cor. 7:3-4).

Wives to Their Husbands

"Wives, *submit* to your husbands *as to the Lord.* . . . Now as the church *submits* to Christ, so also wives should *submit* to their husbands *in everything*" (Eph. 5:22, 24).

"Wives, *submit* to your husbands, as is *fitting in the Lord*" (Col. 3:18).

"Likewise, teach the older women to be *reverent* in the way they live, not to be *slanderers* or *addicted to much wine,* but to teach what is *good.* Then they can train the younger women to *love* their husbands and children, to be *self-controlled* and *pure,* to be *busy at home,* to be *kind,* and to be *subject to their husbands,* so that no one will malign the Word of God" (Titus 2:3-5).

"Wives, in the same way be *submissive* to your husbands so that, if any of them do not believe the Word, they may be won over *without talk* by the behavior of their wives, when they see the *purity* and *reverence* of your lives. Your beauty should not come from outward adornment, such as braided hair and the wearing of gold jewelry and fine clothes. Instead, it should be that of your *inner self,* the unfading beauty of a *gentle* and *quiet spirit,* which is of great worth in God's sight" (1 Peter 3:1-4).

Parents to Children

"Fathers, *do not exasperate your children*; instead, bring them up in the training and instruction of the Lord" (Eph. 6:4).

"Fathers, *do not embitter your children,* or they will become discouraged" (Col. 3:21).

Children to Parents

"Children, *obey* your parents in the Lord, for this is right. '*Honor*' your father and mother'—which is the first commandment with a promise—'that it may go well with you and that you may enjoy long life on the earth' (Eph. 6:1-3).

"Children, *obey* your parents in everything, for this pleases the Lord" (Col. 3:20).

Masters (Employers) to Servants (Employees)

"And masters, treat your slaves the same way. *Do not threaten them,* since you know that He who is both their

Master and yours is in heaven, and there is *no favoritism with Him*" (Eph. 6:9).

"Masters, provide your slaves with what is *right* and *fair,* because you know that you also have a Master in heaven" (Col. 4:1).

Slaves (Employees) to Masters (Employers)

"Slaves, *obey* your earthly masters with *respect* and *fear,* and with *sincerity of heart,* just as you would *obey* Christ. *Obey* them *not only to win their favor* when their eye is on you, but like slaves of Christ, doing the will of God from your heart. *Serve wholeheartedly,* as if you were serving the Lord, not men, because you know that the Lord will reward everyone for whatever good he does, whether he is slave or free" (Eph. 6:5-8; see also Col. 3:22-25).

"Slaves, *submit* yourselves to your masters with all *respect,* not only to those who are good and considerate, but also to those who are harsh" (1 Peter 2:18).

Christians to Government Officials

"Everyone must *submit* himself to the governing authorities, for there is no authority except that which God has established. . . . Therefore, it is necessary to *submit* to the authorities, not only because of possible punishment but also because of conscience. . . . Give everyone what you owe him: If you owe *taxes,* pay taxes; if *revenue,* then revenue; if *respect,* then respect; if *honor,* then honor" (Rom. 13:1, 5, 7).

"*Submit* yourselves for the Lord's sake to *every authority* instituted among men: whether to the *king* as the supreme authority, or to *governors,* who are sent by Him to punish those who do wrong and to commend those who do right. For it is God's will that by doing good you should silence the ignorant talk of foolish men. Live as free men, but do not use your freedom as a cover-up for evil; *live as servants of God.* Show proper *respect* to everyone: *Love* the brotherhood of believers, *fear* God, *honor* the king" (1 Peter 2:13-17).

Step 4

Now that you have isolated your strengths and weaknesses, go back and number the areas where you need improvement. Give yourself a number one in the area of greatest weakness; a number two in the next area, etc.

Now you are ready to set goals for yourself. To begin with, select two areas—one where you are weakest and one where you are strongest. Set up two specific goals—two specific action steps you are going to take to become more obedient to Jesus Christ. Select two new areas each week and set a new goal until you have covered them all.

Keep reviewing and reminding yourself of your previous goals. Pray continually that God will help you obey His Word in these areas.

12

Encourage One Another

"Therefore *encourage one another* and build each other up" (1 Thes. 5:11).

The Apostle Paul had one important concern that was constantly on his mind and heart—to do all he could when he could to build up the body of Christ. And knowing he could only do so much as an individual, his strategy was to transfer this concern to others—to encourage *every other Christian* to develop the same concern for *all other Christians* (Col. 2:2; 4:8).

Paul's concern, of course, forms the basic purpose of this book: to provide believers with biblical and practical guidelines for developing a functioning church. In short, to help Christians build up and edify one another.

As with Paul in the first century, no one Christian in the 20th century can build up all other believers in a local church. God's design and plan is that *every Christian* be a functioning part of the body of Christ; that every Christian contribute to the process. "The whole body," wrote Paul, must be "joined and held together by *every* supporting ligament." And as the body draws strength and direction from its Head, Jesus Christ, it then "grows and builds itself up in love, as each part does its work" (Eph. 4:15-16).

Paul's directive to the Thessalonian Christians, near the end of his first letter to this dynamic New Testament church, is an appropriate exhortation with which to conclude our study. "Therefore, encourage one another and *build each other up*." And then he added, "just as in fact you are doing" (1 Thes. 5:11).

Here was a "functioning" church. Though they were facing severe trials and persecutions (1 Thes. 1:6), and though they were yet to face the trauma of doctrinal disturbance (2 Thes. 2:1-4), Paul commended them for their concern and love for one another. They had learned the importance of mutual encouragement, exhortation, and comfort. Thus Paul commended them, but encouraged them to continue.

The basic Greek word, *parakaleo*, used in 1 Thes. 5:11, appears in several forms in the New Testament. At times the word is translated "to exhort, to admonish, or to teach"; at other times, "to beg, entreat, or beseech." It is also translated "to console; to encourage; to comfort."

But the basic word is always used for one primary purpose —to describe functions that will help Christians to be built up in Christ, or to help them to build up one another in Christ. It is the latter meaning that is in mind in this final chapter. And it is this meaning that Paul had in mind when he exhorted the Thessalonian Christians to "encourage one another and build each other up."

The Primary Means for Encouraging One Another

Paul particularly made it apparent what constituted the primary means for mutual encouragement—God's truth! This is why he wrote to the Ephesian Christians, encouraging them to continue "speaking the truth in love." Then he said, "we will in all things grow up into Him who is the Head, that is, Christ" (Eph. 4:15).

Many biblical examples demonstrate that the primary means for encouraging other believers focuses in God's truth. For example, Paul, giving the qualities for eldership in his letter to Titus, emphasized that a pastoral leader "must hold firmly to the *trustworthy message* as it has been taught, so that he can *encourage others by sound doctrine* and refute those who oppose it" (Titus 1:9).

When he wrote to Timothy, he charged this young minister: "*Preach the Word*; be prepared in season and out of season; correct, rebuke and *encourage*—with great patience and careful instruction" (2 Tim. 4:2). Furthermore, when Paul, Silas, and Timothy discipled the new Christians at Thessalonica, they dealt with each one of them, just as a "father deals with his own children, *encouraging, comforting*, and *urging* [them] to live lives worthy of God" (1 Thes. 2:11-12).

Paul went on to make clear what the means was for encouraging them to live lives worthy of God: "We also thank God continually because, when you received the *Word of God*, which you heard from us, you accepted it not as the word of men, but as it actually is, *the Word of God,* which *is* at work in you who believe" (1 Thes. 2:13).

The Thessalonian Example
The Christians in Thessalonica illustrate the process of mutual encouragement by means of God's Word probably more significantly than any other New Testament church. Let's look at the specific ways in which this encouragement is demonstrated.

1. *The truths regarding the "dead in Christ"*
Even though Paul had instructed the Thessalonian Christians specifically regarding the second coming of Christ (2

Thes. 2:5), they were still confused about those who had died. Somehow they got the impression that those who had passed away may not go to be with the Lord when He comes again. Thus Paul wrote to clarify the issue: "Brothers, we do not want you to be ignorant about those who sleep, or to grieve like the rest of men, who have no hope. We believe that Jesus died and rose again and so we believe that God will bring with Jesus those who sleep in Him" (1 Thes. 4:13-14).

Paul went on to explain thoroughly how this would happen: "The dead in Christ will rise first. After that, we who are still alive and are left will be caught up with them in the clouds to meet the Lord in the air. And so we will be with the Lord forever" (1 Thes. 4:16-17).

And then Paul added this very important exhortation— "Therefore, *encourage each other with these words*" (4:18). In other words, build one another up with this marvelous truth. Remind each other of God's promises. Comfort one another with the fact that *all* believers will spend eternity with Jesus Christ, even though they may die before He comes again. Use God's truth to provide one another with assurance and security.

This, of course, was important to these believers. Some of them—along with New Testament believers elsewhere— actually faced the threat of death because of their faith. How frustrating it must have been to be waiting for Christ's return, not knowing that if they were killed or died naturally before He returned, that they would go to be with Christ just as those who were still alive.

2. *The truth regarding the Rapture of the church*

The Thessalonians had yet another problem. They knew that the day of the Lord—the day of judgment and wrath— was coming upon the earth. And they knew it would "come like a thief in the night" (1 Thes. 5:2). But they evidently did not know what would happen to them before this great and terrible time would come. Thus Paul proceeded to clarify God's truth about the matter. With great assurance in his own heart he wrote: "For God did not appoint us to suffer wrath but to receive salvation through our Lord Jesus Christ. He died for us so that, whether we are awake or asleep, we may live together with Him" (1 Thes. 5:9-10). And then he added another significant exhortation: "Therefore, *encourage one another* and build each other up" (5:11).

Here again Paul encouraged them with God's divine perspective—with God's truth. Then he directed them to "encourage *one another*" with this same truth.

It was this truth that would help build up the body of Christ at Thessalonica. It was this truth that would provide them with stability and assurance as they faced their present trials and the uncertainty of their immediate future. And it was this kind of truth that would enable them to "become mature, attaining the full measure of perfection found in Christ" (Eph. 4:13). And it was no doubt this kind of truth that Paul was referring to when he wrote to the Ephesians: "Then we will no longer be infants, tossed back and forth by the waves, and blown here and there by every wind of teaching and by the cunning and craftiness of men in their deceitful scheming" (Eph. 4:14). In other words, false teaching creates instability and insecurity. God's Word leads to maturity.

3. *The truth regarding the day of the Lord*

The Thessalonian Christians were very vulnerable in the area of eschatology. Satan made this doctrine a key point of attack in their lives. After Paul wrote his first letter, reassuring them regarding the dead in Christ and the rapture of the church that would deliver them from the wrath of God, a false teacher unsettled them, teaching them that "the day of the Lord" had already come (2 Thes. 2:2). Paul immediately wrote a second letter, reassuring them that the day of the

Lord had *not* come. He reminded them of their conversion experience—that God had chosen them "to be saved through the sanctifying work of the Spirit and through *belief in the truth.*" God had called them to "share in the glory of our Lord Jesus Christ"—that is, in His coming (2:13-14).

Paul ended his exposition of God's perspective on the matter with a rather familiar ring in his Thessalonian epistle: "So then, brothers, *stand firm* and *hold to the teachings* we passed on to you, whether by word of mouth or by letter. May our Lord Jesus Christ Himself and God our Father, who loved us and by His grace gave us *eternal encouragement* and good hope, *encourage* and *strengthen* you in every good deed and word" (2:15-17).

Here again we see Paul using God's truth to encourage the Thessalonians. Interestingly, he refers to *"eternal* encouragement." This, of course, is what makes God's Word so powerful, so significant, so reassuring. We are not sharing human philosophy or temporal concepts and ideas that are limited to space and time. Rather, Jesus said, "Heaven and earth will pass away, but My words will never pass away" (Matt. 24:35). This is why God's Word is to be the primary means Christians are to use to "encourage one another" and "to build one another up."

Practical Steps for Helping Christians Encourage One Another
Step 1
All Christians must realize how important the Word of God is in building up others within the body of Christ. And all Christians must be challenged to learn what God's Word says. They must be ready to share the Word with others who are in special need of encouragement. In other words, Christians cannot mutually encourage one another with Scripture if they are not familiar with Scripture. Therefore, encourage each believer in your church to study the Word of God—not

only for personal growth, but to be able to assist others in their growth.

Step 2

Evaluate your church structure in view of this New Testament exhortation. Many traditional churches are designed not for "body function" but for "preacher function." Only the pastor or minister or some other teacher is delegated to share the Word of God with others in the church. Some pastors insist on being the only interpreter of Scripture in the church. The Bible teaches that every Christian must be involved in this process. All Christians are to "speak the truth in love."

Don't misunderstand! It is not wrong for a pastor or teacher to open the Word of God through an extended exposition and message. In fact, this is good, right, and necessary. It was one means in the New Testament for teaching and preaching. But it was not the only means. In fact, more emphasis is placed in Scripture on mutual and informal teaching than on individual and formal communication. This probably is what the author of the Hebrew letter had in mind when he wrote "Let us consider how we may spur *one another* on toward love and good deeds. Let us not give up meeting *together,* as some are in the habit of doing, but let us *encourage one another*—and all the more as you see the Day approaching" (Heb. 10:24-25).

Christians in New Testament days met together for the body of Christ to function—to mutually encourage each other. Though there was certainly formal teaching, there was also informal teaching. This is why Paul wrote to the Colossians, "Let the *Word of Christ* dwell in you richly as you *teach and counsel one another* with all wisdom" (Col. 3:16).

In many of our 20th-century churches, we need to re-evaluate our church structures in the light of New Testament principles and exhortations. Many patterns and approaches are so tightly structured that only what is planned can happen. This stifles the creative ministry of the Holy Spirit. It also causes many Christians to become very dependent on a pastor or, at the most, on leaders to take the responsibility for encouragement and exhortation.

What about your church? What are the patterns like? Is there freedom for every member of the body of Christ to function—"to encourage one another" and "to build one another up"?

Moving from Principles to Patterns

As I conclude this chapter—and this book—I'd like to share a personal experience. Several years ago, after being a professor for nearly 20 years, first at the Moody Bible Institute and later at Dallas Theological Seminary, I helped start a new church in Dallas, Texas. I'd been studying the New Testament church for several years prior to that time. In fact, I had written a book entitled *Sharpening the Focus of the Church*— a study of New Testament church principles. Several Christians in Dallas heard that I had written the book and that it was in the process of being published. They asked me to share these principles in a small home meeting. I did. Among the principles I shared was the importance of "body function" as embodied in the "one another" concepts which I have developed at length in this present volume.[1]

What happened as a result of that meeting somewhat surprised me. That very evening they wanted to start a church— a church that would build structures and patterns upon what we believed were New Testament principles. One of those principles was that there is no such thing as an absolute form

---

[1] In *Sharpening the Focus of the Church* I merely outlined the "one another" concepts on two pages in the chapter entitled "Body Function." In this book, *Building Up One Another*, I have presented these concepts in depth with suggestions for practicing the "one another" principles in a local church.

or pattern for the church. Rather, God gives us principles to guide us. He then sets us free to develop structures that are relevant to a particular culture at any given moment in history.

To make a rather long story short, let me quickly bring you up to date on what has happened. We did start a church. We did develop creative forms. My plan at that time was to just help start it—and then to continue my full-time teaching ministry at the seminary. But God had other plans—for me particularly. We immediately experienced a minor explosion in interest and growth. And today—four years after the publication of *Sharpening the Focus of the Church*, we now have four separate congregations that meet in one building. We have also started three branch churches in the Dallas area. We are planning for several more. Our full-time staff for the four churches which meet in one building now totals eight. We purchased an existing building which seats 300 people. We have built two additional buildings for cash—one which houses our Learning Center for children and another to serve as an office complex for our staff. Because we are now making multiple use of the buildings and investing our money primarily in people, rather than in additional buildings, we are now able—as of this writing—to give 25% of our gross receipts to missions. Hopefully we'll be able to reach 50% in the next couple of years.

In a sense, all that I have described is form. You cannot find it in the New Testament. It is cultural. But we believe it's built upon biblical functions and principles. What we have done represents freedom to be what God wants us to be in the light of New Testament principles. At the heart of these principles stand the "one another" concepts—the concepts developed in this book. Yes, we have formal teaching, but we also have time scheduled for the body of Christ to function—to build itself up.

Let me conclude by illustrating how this can work. In our situation each congregation meets once a week for two and a half hours. (We now have a Friday night congregation, a Sunday morning congregation, a Sunday afternoon congregation, and a Sunday evening congregation. And we are planning a Saturday night congregation.) Our first hour usually is a formal teaching period—formal in the sense that someone opens the Word of God for an extensive period of time. The second hour, following a coffee break in which we fellowship together, is what we call a fellowship and sharing service. Led by one of our elders or pastors, anyone in the church is permitted to participate—by sharing personal prayer needs, by sharing answers to prayer, by sharing Scripture, by requesting songs, by sharing special music (which is usually planned ahead of time), etc. The results have been exciting. And the ministry to one another is very edifying. In fact, as a full-time pastor (I still teach part-time at Dallas Theological Seminary) I usually sit through four different sharing services each weekend, but never grow tired of the experience. My life is constantly edified by other members of the body of Christ.

Let me explain with this final illustration: In one of the churches I noticed a man walk in who had not been present for many months. I knew he was having a moral problem. I was probably the only one present who paid particular attention to his being there and one of the very few who knew he had a problem. As a body, we "happened" to be sharing Scripture with one another. To my amazement, one after another, people stood up and shared Scripture that had a direct bearing on this man's problem. Those who shared, of course, knew nothing of this man's situation. But the Holy Spirit did —and on one of those rare occasions, I was allowed to see God at work in a dramatic way through various members of Christ's body.

I firmly believe that this kind of experience should not be a rare one. Rather, our 20th-century churches should be structured so that it can happen regularly. And if we will only study the principles of Scripture and develop patterns that are biblically and culturally related, I believe God will do great things through His people.

If you were to ask me why this work has grown and expanded so rapidly, I would not be able to give you a simple answer. One thing I'm sure of, however: It's been a result of many factors—both human and divine. A study of history has taught me that no one man can take credit for God's doing.

One thing stands out as being very important in this ministry—the "body of Christ." *Every member* contributes to its success. It has been a corporate effort by a group of people who believe the Bible, who believe in the God of the Bible, who love and care for "one another," and who want all men to be saved and to experience fellowship with God and with other believers. This is a dynamic that God has promised to bless. This dynamic is what Jesus prayed for when He was yet on earth. And with that prayer I conclude: "My prayer is not for them alone. I pray also for those who will believe in Me through their message, that all of them may be one, Father, just as You are in Me and I am in You. May they also be in Us so that the world may believe that You have sent Me. I have given them the glory that You gave Me, that they may be one as We are one: I in them and You in Me. May they be brought to complete unity to let the world know that You sent Me and have loved them even as You have loved me" (John 17:20-23).